D0889706

TASTING

PARIS

TASTING
PARIS

100 RECIPES TO EAT LIKE A LOCAL

CLOTILDE DUSOULIER

CLARKSON POTTER/PUBLISHERS
NEW YORK

COPYRIGHT © 2018 BY CLOTILDE DUSOULIER
PHOTOGRAPHS COPYRIGHT © 2018
BY NICOLE FRANZEN

ALL RIGHTS RESERVED.
PUBLISHED IN THE UNITED STATES BY
CLARKSON POTTER/PUBLISHERS,
AN IMPRINT OF THE CROWN PUBLISHING
GROUP, A DIVISION OF PENGUIN RANDOM
HOUSE LLC, NEW YORK.

CROWNPUBLISHING.COM
CLARKSONPOTTER.COM

CLARKSON POTTER IS A TRADEMARK AND
POTTER WITH COLOPHON IS A REGISTERED
TRADEMARK OF PENGUIN RANDOM HOUSE LLC.

THE LIBRARY OF CONGRESS
LC RECORD IS AVAILABLE AT
HTTPS://LCCN.LOC.GOV/2017025780.

ISBN 978-0-451-49914-1
EBOOK ISBN 978-0-451-49915-8

PRINTED IN CHINA

BOOK AND COVER DESIGN BY JEN WANG
COVER PHOTOGRAPHS BY NICOLE FRANZEN

10 9 8 7 6 5 4 3 2 1

FIRST EDITION

FOR ANNE
my favorite honorary Parisian,
who made this so fun

WELCOME TO PARIS

WELCOME TO PARIS

BIENVENUE À PARIS

ON ONE'S FIRST OR PERHAPS EVEN SECOND VISIT TO PARIS, IT'S HARD NOT to be seduced by the city's most famous sights: the monumental avenues such as the Champs-Elysées, which links the Arc de Triomphe and the Place de la Concorde; the Eiffel Tower; Notre-Dame; Place des Vosges. I've lived here all my life, and riding my bicycle across any one of the Seine's bridges still makes my heart swell.

But what I think of most when I wander my hometown is food: Saint-Germain-des-Prés, to me, means macarons from Pierre Hermé and Les Halles roast chicken from the Champeaux brasserie. The Tuileries, bordered on the north by rue de Rivoli, bring to mind Angelina and thus hot chocolate, and the cafés near Porte Dauphine, where I spent my student years, evoke the satisfying croque-madame, the velvety yolk dripping down the crust of the bread. Barbès seduces with couscous; Belleville comforts with Chinese rice soup. From humble stews to sophisticated pastries, vibrant greens to oozy cheeses, the classic to the creative, the familiar to the exotic—it's all here, waiting for you to hop off at the closest metro station, push open a door, and walk in.

There are so many tasty ways a day can unfold in Paris. Will it begin with a flaky croissant dipped in café au lait, or a slice of rye and red miso bread from the city's most innovative baker? At lunch, will you close your eyes in bliss at the first forkful of lettuce, dressed in the perfect bistro vinaigrette? Or will you opt for a Kurdish "pizza" from a sandwich shack at Faubourg-Saint-Denis?

Later in the afternoon, will you stop for black tea with Earl Grey madeleines, or mint tea at the Great Mosque, with orange blossom and date cookies? Next, your Parisian friends may invite you for a predinner drink and surprise you with a classy, timeless cocktail, like a French 75, and the gratinéed mussels they whipped up like it's nothing.

Finally, you'll end the day at a favorite bistro for a soul-warming pot-au-feu, unless you try that exciting new restaurant nobody knows about (yet) where you'll have the best trout. And maybe some profiteroles, if there's room.

Paris is a multifaceted city, with a multitude of cultures and flavors pulsing through its streets. I've captured my favorite recipes here, along with the stories that give them life, to create a snapshot of my city today—to bring a little bit of Paris into your home, and to tide you over between visits.

On y va ?

Find a full directory of the places mentioned, variations for special diets, menus, behind-the-scenes videos, and other free bonuses at tastingpariscookbook.com.

A BRIEF HISTORY
OF
PARISIAN
CUISINE

PARIS WAS ALWAYS DESTINED TO BECOME AN EXCEPTIONAL CITY for food and dining.

In Roman times, and until the fourth century, Paris was called Lutetia. Its position on the Seine, and the proximity of two additional rivers, allowed the town to thrive and grow. The islets at the city's heart—of which Île de la Cité and Île Saint-Louis remain—made it easy to cross the river, aiding commerce.

A vast vineyard—the largest in France until the nineteenth century—enriched the landscape, so Parisians drank local wine and cooked with vinegar. The rich wetlands were ideal for growing produce, and *maraîchers* carted in their fresh salads, herbs, and vegetables daily. Further out, a vast expanse of land was devoted to grain, which was milled and then baked into bread. Easy access to woods and pastures kept the city fed with meat, wild or farmed, and dairy products.

Parisians were self-sufficient, reveling in their unique culinary setting. But the city was also an exceptional hub of power and wealth, and the elite, eager to eat delicacies from other French provinces and far beyond, imported them—first by boat, then through a well-developed road system, and eventually via the railroad. This openness to new and sometimes foreign flavors eventually trickled down to all classes, becoming a notable trait of Parisian cuisine.

Paris is also the birthplace of the restaurant as we know it. In the late eighteenth century, as noble families fled the city in the aftermath of the French Revolution, they left their kitchen staff behind. These highly trained cooks had always practiced their craft in private settings, serving food *à la française*: multiple preparations served all at once to form

Breakfast

Omelettes

Sandwiches

Tartines Poilâne

Snack

Plat du Jour

Formule

a ridiculously bountiful spread. They cast this outdated model aside and opened novel establishments—the first restaurants—where anyone could come in and compose a meal, dish by dish, off a menu. Around the same time, pastry chefs and *charcutiers* opened new shops with large windows displaying spectacular goods to passers-by. This historic change from private to public dining led to the official birth of gastronomy: an elevated appreciation of good food and a field of social study.

In the 1800s, Europeans started to travel more, and outside influences continued to develop the culinary culture of Paris; German-inspired brasseries and *bouillons*—simple restaurants selling affordable foods to the working class—sprang up, for example. This trend continued into the 1900s, as the French left rural provinces to make it in the big city before the great wars. In the decades that followed, migrant populations from Europe, Asia, and Africa followed, each community bringing diversity to the mix and enriching the food scene.

In recent history, two major shifts have affected how Parisians eat: one was the advent of *nouvelle cuisine* in the 1970s, which did away with heavy dishes and rich sauces. It coincided with new concerns over health, nutrition, and even sustainability, which all play an increasing role in dictating what Parisians eat today, and what restaurants serve.

Another historic milestone was the appearance of gastro-bistros in the '90s, when a generation of classically trained young chefs decided to leave fine-dining restaurants and luxury hotels to open bistros of their own. There, they applied their haute cuisine skills to humbler ingredients, making their food affordable for ordinary diners. The dawn of *bistronomie* was a turning point for Paris chefs. It helped reinvigorate the dining landscape as well as liberate home cooks to explore this new, creative style of cooking.

Today, I will argue that the Paris food scene is more exciting, more diverse, more open-minded than it has ever been. In the wake of the 2008 economic crisis, chefs and diners alike have reevaluated what it means to live in a gastronomic capital, and their standards are high. Independence, innovation, playfulness, and multiculturalism are central values, and evolutions in food trends are embraced just as the city's deep-rooted history is honored and celebrated.

MORNING

LE MATIN

Il est cinq heures
Paris s'éveille
—JACQUES DUTRONC

TAKING MY CHILDREN TO SCHOOL EARLY IN THE MORNING
means passing commuters coming in and out of the Art
Nouveau metro station; a bakery, shelves loaded, the warm
smell of croissants wafting out of the sidewalk vents; and a
neighborhood café, where a handful of customers gulp down
espressos at the zinc counter.

I cross paths with other parents nudging along their young
children, street cleaners picking up the traces of the previous
night's parties, employees from the charcuterie around the
corner, and office workers in business attire, adjusting ties and
scarves. It's still quiet but the city is waking up, and if I'm lucky
the sky is pink and blue over Sacré-Coeur.

Days full of promise begin with a good breakfast, and as I
study my fellow Parisians, exchanging smiles with familiar
faces, I wonder secretly about their *petit déjeuner*. A buttered
tartine dunked in *chocolat chaud*? A bowl of cereal with yogurt?
A brioche stashed in their briefcase for later?

Whatever style resonates with you, this chapter presents
delicious options for having breakfast or brunch, Paris-style,
chez vous.

~CAFÉ AU LAIT~
classique

CLASSIC
CAFÉ AU LAIT

SERVES 2

CAFÉ AU LAIT (COFFEE WITH MILK), A FIFTY-FIFTY MIX OF WHOLE MILK and coffee swirling together into a soft and silky morning drink, is a beloved staple of home-style French breakfasts. The trick is to start with very strong coffee, about twice as strong as you would if you were drinking it black, so the flavor of the beans comes through the milkiness. Serving it in a bowl is also key (ideally, a chipped flea market find), so you can dunk your buttered *tartines* or the tip of your croissant.

Note that ordering café au lait at a Parisian café, however perfectly accented your French, is a dead giveaway that you're not from around here. Café au lait is the beverage the French make in the privacy of their own kitchen with drip coffee and heated milk. What you want to order from your café server is a *café crème*, made from an espresso and machine-steamed milk, which will arrive in a proper *tasse*. No dunking allowed.

1½ cups (360 ml) very strong coffee

1½ cups (360 ml) whole milk (or unsweetened unflavored nondairy milk)

Sugar (optional)

· VARIATIONS ·

For a frothy café au lait, buzz the hot milk (carefully) in a blender for a few seconds before pouring, or use the steamer spout of a home espresso machine to heat it up.

Don't drink coffee? Try this with strong instant chicory.

Set out two bowls (or mugs), each about 1½ cups (360 ml) in capacity.

While the coffee is brewing, bring the milk to just under a simmer in a saucepan. Don't allow it to boil. Divide the hot coffee between the two bowls and stir in the hot milk.

Serve immediately, with sugar on the side for those who prefer their coffee sweetened.

IN RECENT YEARS, THE PARIS COFFEE SCENE HAS EXPERIENCED A MUCH-
needed renaissance. Yes, traditional cafés have long been central to the
city's social fabric, but nobody really goes for the coffee. Thankfully, a
younger generation of coffee aficionados, blown away by the craft coffee
they drank in Melbourne, London, or New York, decided French people
deserved fabulous coffee. Now, every neighborhood in Paris has several
indie coffee shops that can be trusted to deliver a fine cup—and some
inventive fare; my favorite in Montmartre is Cuillier, which is popular
with local freelancers who come in the morning to start their day off right.
If they're hungry for breakfast, they may opt for this poached egg and
yogurt bowl, topped with bread crumbs and onion pickle. An intriguing
combination of ingredients, I agree, but a surprisingly successful one.

~ŒUFS POCHÉS~
chapelure et oignon
en aigre-doux

POACHED EGGS
WITH BREAD CRUMBS & ONION PICKLE

SERVES 4

· **NOTE** ·
It's important that the eggs be
very fresh because the yolk is not
cooked through when poached.

· **VARIATION** ·
Serve over wilted spinach or a
boiled sweet potato.

1 tablespoon unsalted butter
or rendered bacon fat

½ cup (50 g) unseasoned bread
crumbs (see Making Your
Own Bread Crumbs, page 18)

1 tablespoon vinegar

Fine sea salt

4 large eggs (see Note),
cold from the refrigerator

1½ cups (360 ml) plain full-fat
Greek yogurt, preferably
at room temperature

Freshly ground black pepper

Quick Red Onion Pickle
(recipe follows)

In a small skillet, melt the butter over medium heat. Add the bread
crumbs, stir to coat, and cook, stirring regularly, until lightly browned,
3 to 4 minutes. Transfer to a bowl.

Fill a medium saucepan halfway up with water. Add the vinegar and
½ teaspoon salt and bring to a boil, then reduce the heat so that the
water is just under a simmer. You want water that is as hot as possible
without being so bubbly and agitated that the egg white strands will
disperse.

Break one egg into a ladle. Lower the ladle into the pan, keeping
it against the side so the egg remains contained in these first few
moments. Remove the ladle and let the egg cook for 3 minutes without
disturbing (4 to 5 if you prefer a firmer yolk). Lift the egg out with a
slotted spoon and reserve on a plate. Repeat with the remaining eggs.
(Poaching eggs takes a little practice; don't get discouraged if they don't
come out perfect the first time.)

Divide the yogurt among 4 shallow bowls. Add a poached egg to each,
and season with salt and pepper. Sprinkle with the bread crumbs, top
with a few slices of pickle, and serve.

MAKING YOUR OWN BREAD CRUMBS

If you buy good bread and have a blender or food processor, there is no need to purchase bread crumbs, ever. Allow leftover pieces of bread to dry completely in a bowl on the counter, and process until finely ground (this is very loud but effective). Don't worry if the grind is uneven. Transfer to an airtight container, keep at room temperature, and use within 3 months.

QUICK RED ONION PICKLE

Oignon rouge en aigre-doux

MAKES ABOUT 1½ CUPS (360 ML)

THIS QUICK PICKLE FORMULA transforms a red onion into the prettiest pink slivers to boost savory breakfast bowls, salads, roasted vegetables, and sandwiches with delightful notes of sweet, sour, and crunchy pungency.

1 medium red onion (about 8 ounces/225 g), peeled

3 cups (720 ml) boiling water

1 cup (240 ml) white wine vinegar or cider vinegar

1 tablespoon sugar

1 teaspoon fine sea salt

2 teaspoons spices, such as black or pink peppercorns, coriander seeds, cumin seeds, or juniper berries (optional)

· **VARIATION** ·

Add a small, thinly sliced fresh red chile to the jar, interspersed with the onion rings.

Have ready a spotlessly clean, 1½-cup (360 ml) glass jar with a tight-fitting lid.

Using a sharp knife or mandoline, cut the onion into slices ⅛ inch (4 mm) thick, working your way from stem end to root. Put the onion slices in a metal colander in the sink, separating the slices into rings.

Pour the boiling water over the onions rings. Pack them into the jar.

In a small saucepan, combine the vinegar, sugar, salt, and spices (if using) and bring to a simmer, stirring to dissolve the sugar and salt. Pour into the jar, tamp the onion rings down so they're fully immersed, and close the lid. Cool on the counter completely before using, 1 to 2 hours.

Store the leftovers in the refrigerator up to 1 month. The pickle will improve further over the next 2 days.

~PAIN AU CACAO~
et chocolat

CHOCOLATE
BREAD

**MAKES THREE 12-OUNCE
(340 G) LOAVES**

18th, a typical Paris market street that defies logic by featuring half a dozen successful *boulangeries*, some of them just one block apart. Such is the luxury of Parisians, to be able to elect their corner bakery among many. Mine is Maison Landemaine, which offers a divine chocolate bread. This is not to be confused with *pain au chocolat,* which is croissant dough wrapped around two sticks of chocolate. I'm talking about a yeasted bread flavored with cocoa powder and studded with chocolate chips. Not too sweet and not too rich, it makes a perfect beginning to the day, lightly toasted and spread with butter or almond butter.

This recipe makes three medium loaves; I suggest you eat one now, gift the second, and freeze the third. (There's a life lesson in there somewhere.)

· **NOTE** ·

The overnight rest helps develop flavor and makes the process easier to fit into your schedule.

· **VARIATION** ·

Add dried cherries or roasted hazelnuts to the dough.

2¼ teaspoons active dry yeast

2¼ cups (540 ml) lukewarm water

5¼ cups (680 g) bread flour, plus more for dusting

½ cup (60 g) unsweetened Dutch-process cocoa powder

2 tablespoons (25 g) sugar

2 teaspoons fine sea salt

5 ounces (140 g) bittersweet chocolate chips (60 to 70% cacao), or chopped chocolate

Prepare the dough the day before baking. Proof the yeast in 1 cup (240 ml) of the lukewarm water (see How to Proof Yeast, opposite).

In the bowl of a stand mixer fitted with the dough hook (or in a large bowl if working by hand), stir together the flour, cocoa powder, sugar, salt, yeast mixture, and remaining 1¼ cups (300 ml) lukewarm water until combined. Knead with the dough hook on medium-low speed for 5 minutes (if working by hand, transfer to the counter and knead for 10 minutes), until the dough is smooth and pulls away from the sides of the bowl or counter. Add the chocolate chips and knead just to distribute. (If working by hand, return to the bowl.) Cover the bowl with a kitchen towel and let rest for 1 hour at room temperature in a draft-free corner of the kitchen.

After this rest, "fold" the dough about twelve times in the bowl, pulling it up from the sides and over itself with a spatula. This develops flavor and creates a well-structured crumb. Cover the bowl with plastic wrap and refrigerate for 8 to 12 hours, at your convenience.

The next day, remove the dough from the fridge; it should have doubled in size. Remove the plastic wrap and cover the bowl with a kitchen towel. Let the dough come back to room temperature, about 1 hour.

Line a baking sheet with parchment paper. Scrape the dough onto a well-floured surface and divide into 3 equal pieces. To shape each into a bâtard, or oval loaf, first flatten into a round about 8 inches (20 cm) in

⩙ HOW TO PROOF YEAST

To activate your yeast, you need to proof it first. In a bowl, combine the yeast with the lukewarm water listed in the recipe. Set aside for 10 minutes, until foamy at the surface. If it doesn't get foamy, the yeast is likely too old; start again with a fresh packet.

diameter; if the dough is stiff, use your fist to pound it into submission. Now imagine the round as a clock face: Picking up the dough from 10 and 2, pull both edges in and overlap in the center to form a narrow triangle, pointy end at the top. Switch the dough around so the pointy end points toward you, and roll up the triangle gently but firmly, starting from the pointy end, tucking the free sides in until you reach the end.

Transfer to the baking sheet, spacing the loaves a few inches apart, and let rest for 30 minutes.

Preheat the oven to 450°F (230°C).

Slash the top of each loaf three times with a baker's blade or sharp knife, holding the blade at an angle. Bake in the middle of the oven until the loaves sound hollow when tapped on the bottom, 40 to 45 minutes, rotating the sheet front to back after 30 minutes.

Transfer to a rack to cool completely before eating. (The bread will be gummy and underwhelming if you slice it too soon.)

IF YOU WERE TO SNEAK INTO A PARISIAN HOME AND OPEN THE REFRIGERATOR, there is one thing you would find for certain: yogurt. A lot of it. *Yaourt* is so important to the French diet that it's almost its own food group; the variety offered by any supermarket spans multiple aisles—and that's just for plain, unsweetened yogurt. If you want to get into the flavored stuff, well, we may be here a while. Beyond simple fruit flavors and standard options (berries, stone fruits, tropical fruits; chunky, smooth, jam at the bottom), a whole range of dessert-inspired flavors have taken the market by storm, including tarte tatin, chocolate macaron, salted butter caramel, strawberry charlotte . . .

I prefer plain yogurt myself, and love it at breakfast with a seasonal fruit compote such as this one, poached in tea and sweetened with honey. I prepare a big batch on the weekend and draw from it throughout the week. In summer, I opt for peaches, apricots, and cherries and in fall and winter apples, pears, and plums or grapes. Use this formula with any combination of fruits; it's a good way to upcycle imperfect ones sold at a reduced price.

~COMPOTE DE FRUITS~
au thé et au miel, yaourt

TEA & HONEY
FRUIT
COMPOTE
WITH YOGURT

SERVES 6

1 tablespoon loose-leaf tea of your choice (green, black, or rooibos)

¼ cup (85 g) honey

2 pounds (900 g) mixed seasonal fruits

Plain full-fat yogurt (dairy or nondairy), for serving

Bring 2 cups (480 ml) water to a boil and steep the tea in it following the package or seller's instructions. Strain into a large saucepan and stir in the honey until dissolved.

Meanwhile, prepare the fruits: Peel them as needed, remove the pits or cores, and cut into 1-inch (2.5 cm) wedges or cubes. Add half of the fruits to the tea in the pan. Bring to a low simmer over medium heat and cook, stirring from time to time, until the fruits are soft and cooked through but not falling apart, 3 to 15 minutes depending on the nature and ripeness of the fruits.

Using a slotted spoon, scoop the fruits into a serving bowl (or glass container with a lid if making ahead). Repeat the simmering process with the remaining fruits. Combine all of the simmered fruits together. Cool on the counter, then cover and refrigerate for 3 to 4 days. (The remaining tea can be strained and chilled for a fruity iced tea.)

Serve the compote cold or at room temperature, with a dollop of yogurt.

BREAKFAST & BRUNCH

IN PARIS AS IN MOST OF THE COUNTRY, BREAKFAST IS THOUGHT OF AS A private meal, taken at home. Rarely is any cooking involved: We will sit at our (tiny) kitchen tables to eat toast spread with butter or jam, a bowl of cold cereal with milk, or fruit and yogurt (see page 23).

For those who failed to wake up on time, cafés keep a basket of fresh croissants on the bar throughout the morning, and customers can help themselves to one as they stand at the counter drinking an espresso. When the croissant basket is empty, a waiter will (literally) run out to the closest bakery and have them fill it back up.

If you prefer a sit-down breakfast, cafés usually offer a couple of set menus, the simplest including a croissant, fresh baguette with butter and jam, coffee or tea, and orange juice. Bigger appetites will go for the continental breakfast that adds a fried egg with ham.

What about brunch? Still considered a thrilling novelty in the early naughts, brunch was enthusiastically adopted by Parisians. But it took a good decade for restaurants to grasp the concept and start doing brunch properly, i.e., not just selling overpriced eggs and salads of leftovers.

There is now a multitude of places to go on weekend mornings for tasty egg and brunchy dishes, served generously and often buffet-style. It's exciting to witness the Frenchification of the format, as endive salads, roast chicken, aged cheeses, quiches, crêpes, brioches, and croquemadames invite themselves to the party.

~BRIOCHE~
du matin

MORNING
BRIOCHE

**MAKES 12 BRIOCHE BUNS
OR 2 FLOWER-SHAPED
BRIOCHES**

PARIS IS AN EMBARRASSMENT OF BRIOCHE RICHES. AVAILABLE FROM ANY corner bakery, this buttery bread comes in every shape and size, from single-serving buns to brioches baked in ribbed tins with cute little heads; plain or flavored with orange blossom water; topped with pearl sugar or studded with chocolate chips. I am a fan of the simplest ones: single-serving buns with a sprinkling of sugar on top.

Brioche dough benefits from a night's rest in the fridge, so you can prep it the evening before, then shape and bake in the morning. By the time everyone is showered and ready to go (or the minute your brunch guests press the buzzer), the yeasty, buttery scent of brioche fills the air, and golden buns sit glowingly on the table.

· NOTES ·

The dough may be frozen after shaping: Put the whole sheet(s) in the freezer for 2 hours, then transfer the dough to a freezer bag. Before baking, put the dough on a sheet of parchment paper to thaw overnight in the refrigerator.

Alternatively, you can freeze the brioches after baking and cooling. To serve, thaw overnight in the refrigerator and pop in a 350°F (175°C) oven for 5 minutes to restore the texture.

These practically beg for a smear of Quick Blackberry Jam (page 40) or Chocolate Hazelnut Spread (page 43).

The next day, leftover brioche can be toasted or turned into Blackberry Bostock (page 39).

2¼ teaspoons active dry yeast

¼ cup (60 ml) lukewarm water

3 cups (400 g) all-purpose flour

½ cup (100 g) sugar

1 teaspoon fine sea salt,
plus a pinch for the egg wash

5 large eggs

12 tablespoons (170 g) unsalted
butter, diced, at room temperature

Pearl sugar, for sprinkling
(optional)

Start preparing the dough the day before serving. Proof the yeast in the lukewarm water (see How to Proof Yeast, page 21).

In the bowl of a stand mixer fitted with the dough hook, combine the flour, yeast mixture, sugar, and salt. Add 4 of the eggs and knead on low speed until smooth, about 2 minutes. Switch to medium speed and knead until the dough pulls away from the sides of the bowl, about 2 minutes. Add the butter piece by piece and knead until incorporated, about 2 minutes, scraping the sides of the bowl regularly. (You can knead by hand on the countertop; it just takes persistence, as this is a sticky dough. Plan to knead for 10 minutes before incorporating the butter, and 10 minutes after. Scrape into a bowl when done.)

Cover the bowl and let the dough rise at room temperature in a draft-free corner of the kitchen until doubled in size, 1½ to 2 hours.

Cover the bowl with plastic wrap and refrigerate for 8 to 12 hours, at your convenience.

The next day, remove the dough from the refrigerator. Line two baking sheets with parchment paper.

In a bowl, lightly beat the remaining egg with a pinch of salt and 2 teaspoons water; this is your egg wash.

Scrape the dough onto a lightly floured work surface. Divide the dough into 12 pieces and, with lightly floured hands, shape each into a ball. For brioche buns, transfer to the baking sheets, placing the balls 2 inches (5 cm) apart. For two flower-shaped brioches, form a flower shape on each baking sheet: Place a ball in the middle of each sheet and push 5 more around it snugly.

Brush off the excess flour from the top and sides and brush with the egg wash (reserve the remaining egg wash in the refrigerator). Allow the brioches to rest at room temperature for 30 minutes.

Preheat the oven to 350°F (175°C).

Brush with egg wash again and sprinkle with pearl sugar if desired. Bake until golden brown, about 15 minutes for brioche buns and 20 to 25 minutes for the flower-shaped brioches, switching the position of the sheets top to bottom and back to front halfway through.

Transfer to a rack to cool. Serve slightly warm or at room temperature.

· **VARIATIONS** ·

Fold 1 cup (160 g) high-quality chocolate chips into the dough after kneading and omit the pearl sugar.

Use just 3 whole eggs and 1 yolk in the dough, and add 3 tablespoons orange blossom water when mixing them in.

LA MAISON POILÂNE

THE PARIS BREAD SCENE WOULD NOT BE WHAT IT IS TODAY WITHOUT THE vision and hard work of the Poilâne family.

A second-generation baker, Lionel Poilâne took over his father's bakery on rue du Cherche-Midi in the seventies. Like his father, Pierre, he was appalled by the whiter-than-white bread that consumers had favored since the end of World War II, as a symbol of peacetime and abundance.

On the contrary, Lionel was adamantly attached to the *miche Poilâne*, a sourdough loaf big enough to hug that Pierre had developed in the early thirties using stone-ground, unrefined flour and baked in the ancient wood-burning oven that's down a steep, slippery stairwell from the Saint-Germain-des-Prés shop.

Lionel ran the business ingeniously for three decades, developing the brand overseas and expanding production while maintaining the bakery's artisanal mission. And when Parisians started to catch on to the blandness and nutritional vacuum of white bread, the Poilâne bakery was right there, waiting for them.

Lionel Poilâne died in a tragic accident with his wife, Irena, in 2002. Their eldest daughter Apollonia, then only eighteen, took over with remarkable aplomb and has been running the company ever since. Now at the helm of six shops in Paris, London, and Antwerp, she has followed in her father's footsteps, keeping the product range tight and narrow, and only introducing her creations—a spoon-shaped butter cookie to stir your coffee, a honey spice cake, a granola bar—after careful deliberation.

There is something luminously Parisian about this less-is-more philosophy, and the Maison Poilâne is a standard by which every bakery in Paris is judged. For anyone passionate about artisanal bread and family-run businesses, the Cherche-Midi boutique is a must-visit spot in Paris with tons of history and Old World charm.

I myself have been a customer since I was a little girl, when my father took my sister and me to get our weekly *miche* on Saturday mornings. I recommend you get a quarter of the legendary loaf, but don't overlook the rye bread (my favorite), and sample a *punition* (butter cookie) from the basket by the register. It tastes like my childhood.

farine de blé moulue à la meule de pierre,
eau, sel de Guérande

Miche Décorée avec Inscription
Poids : 2,1 kg / Prix pièce : 29,85 €
Sur commande

farine de blé moulue à la meule de pierre,
eau, sel de Guérande

Miche Po
4,90 € /

~BAGHRIRS~

MOROCCAN CRUMPETS

MAKES 16 CRUMPETS

ALSO CALLED CRÊPES MILLE-TROUS ("ONE-THOUSAND-HOLE PANCAKES"), *baghrirs* are a popular treat across North Africa, especially during Ramadan. During this holy month of fasting, Muslims in Paris and around the world refrain from eating and drinking from sunup until sundown. When night sets in, friends and relatives gather to break the fast together with a great big feast. In families with roots in Morocco, Algeria, or Tunisia, the tables will likely be loaded with *chorba* (lamb soup), *pastilla* (a flaky pigeon pie), couscous and tagines (see pages 198 and 88), and a platter of baghrirs, looking like cousins of the British crumpet. These simple, yeast-leavened pancakes are cooked in a skillet on just one side, as bubbles pierce the surface to form one thousand (give or take) holes. They have a lightly nubby texture from the use of fine semolina flour, and are served warm, with melted butter and honey, to be rolled up and eaten with the tips of the fingers.

In the spirit of "breaking fast," these North African pancakes are a delight for breakfast or brunch.

· NOTE ·
While the traditional baghrir is leavened with yeast only, contemporary cooks use this formula, which includes baking powder and requires only a short resting period.

2¼ teaspoons active dry yeast

½ cup (120 ml) lukewarm water

1¼ cup (200 g) fine-grind semolina
(also sold as semolina flour)

1½ teaspoons baking powder

¼ teaspoon fine sea salt

3 large eggs

3 tablespoons (55 g) honey

4 tablespoons (55 g)
unsalted butter

Neutral oil, such as grapeseed
or canola

Start 1 hour before serving. Proof the yeast in the lukewarm water (see
How to Proof Yeast, page 21).

In a medium bowl, combine the semolina, baking powder, and salt
(see Note). Whisk in the yeast mixture, eggs, and ¼ cup (60 ml) cold
water until you get a creamy batter, not too thick but not too runny,
kind of like pancake batter. Add in more water as needed, tablespoon
by tablespoon, to get the right consistency. Cover and let rest at room
temperature for 30 minutes.

In a small saucepan, melt together the honey and butter over low heat,
whisking to combine.

Heat a large skillet over medium heat. Add ½ teaspoon oil and spread
across the bottom of the skillet with a wadded-up paper towel to absorb
the excess fat (watch your fingers). Keep the paper towel in a cup by
the stove.

Using a small ladle, pour about 3 tablespoons of batter in the center
of the skillet. Allow it to cook without disturbing as bubbles rise to the
surface, 3 to 5 minutes. The baghrir is cooked when the top is set. Don't
flip it: Baghrirs are only cooked on one side.

Transfer to a plate, cover with a kitchen towel to keep warm, and repeat
with the rest of the batter, oiling the pan again lightly with the paper
towel. Once comfortable with your heat setting, cook 2 or 3 baghrirs at
a time, as many as will fit in your skillet.

Serve warm with the honey butter for drizzling. Cover and keep any
leftovers in the fridge for up to 2 days; reheat gently in a dry skillet or toaster.

THE PARIS CROISSANT

THE SCENE: A TYPICAL PARIS CAFÉ IN EARLY MORNING. A MAN APPROACHES the counter. *"Un express, s'il vous plaît!"* Amid the clang and hiss of the espresso machine, he plucks a croissant from the basket on the bar and downs it in three bites, shielding his tie from the shower of flakes.

Croissants are everywhere in Paris. From the butter-stained paper bag brought in for the first meeting of the day to kids devouring their after-school snack, the golden, crescent-shaped treat is as much a part of the scenery as the Eiffel Tower.

Made with leavened puff pastry, hovering between sweet and savory, a good croissant is a true work of craftsmanship that demands the highest quality of butter and flour, well-honed skills, and time for the dough to develop its flavor. The result is so good it shuts you right up: two irresistibly crunchy tips, a crisp and lightly caramelized outer shell, a moist and creamy crumb, and the clean taste of butter.

The croissant is my measuring stick for judging a bakery: Both an incredibly simple and incredibly complex product, it is most revealing of the artisan's touch.

Sadly, fewer and fewer *boulangers* make croissants from scratch. The process can span up to three days, yet the pastry itself is such a basic necessity that Parisians aren't willing to pay very much for it. Croissants are usually sold at cost, unless the baker opts to buy factory-made and frozen ones to create a higher margin.

An experienced palate will know the difference, or you can call upon your intuition. What's your first impression when you enter the *boulangerie*? Do the offerings have a unified style? Do the staff seem knowledgeable about what they're selling? If so, it's likely you've found your bliss; go ahead and bite in.

PARIS USED TO BE A HOSTILE PLACE FOR VEGETARIANS—LET ALONE VEGANS.
Outside of a handful of vegetarian restaurants, waiters and chefs had no idea what plant-based eating was about. Restaurant menus were devoid of meat-free options, and vegetarians had to settle for a hodgepodge of sides or a bowl of soup.

The Paris food scene experienced a historic shift toward vegetables around the turn of the twentieth century; chef Alain Passard led the charge with a disruptive all-vegetable menu served at his three-star restaurant. It is now common to find inspired vegetarian courses at contemporary bistros, and the city is peppered with restaurants devoted to plant-based dining, the kind where you can take your omnivore friends and not have them notice the absence of meat. Chief among them is gastro-vegan restaurant Le Potager de Charlotte, where a signature appetizer is the *avocat façon œuf mimosa*, a "deviled egg" avocado with turmeric-yellow hummus taking the place of the mashed yolk, and toasted squash seeds for crunch. I serve a bunch of them on a platter, with spoons for eating, for brunch; they look so appetizing and are always the first item to disappear.

1 (15-ounce/400 g) can or jar chickpeas, rinsed and drained (see Note)

2 teaspoons tahini

1 garlic clove

1 teaspoon ground turmeric

Fine sea salt

¼ teaspoon freshly ground black pepper

2 tablespoons freshly squeezed lemon juice, or more to taste

2 tablespoons olive oil

4 avocados (about 6 ounces/ 170 g each), halved and pitted

1 teaspoon smoked or regular paprika

Fleur de sel, for serving

½ cup (115 g) squash seeds, toasted

3 tablespoons finely chopped chives

· **NOTE** ·

To use home-cooked chickpeas, you'll need 1⅓ cups (240 g): Soak ½ cup (110 g) dried chickpeas overnight and cook in a saucepan of boiling water until cooked through and tender, about 1 hour. Drain well.

In a food processor, process the chickpeas, tahini, garlic, turmeric, 1 teaspoon salt, the pepper, lemon juice, oil, and 3 tablespoons water until smooth. Add a little more water, tablespoon by tablespoon, as needed until creamy but still scoopable. Taste and add more salt or lemon juice as needed.

Scoop 2 rounded tablespoons of hummus into each avocado "hole," as for deviled eggs.

Arrange on a serving platter. Sprinkle with the paprika, fleur de sel, squash seeds, and chives.

~PAIN~

de seigle au miso rouge

RYE & RED MISO BREAD

MAKES ONE 14-OUNCE (400 G) LOAF

YOU CAN STILL FIND OLD-SCHOOL, SLEEPY BAKERIES IN PARIS WHERE a chronically irritated *boulangère* sells croissants *ordinaires* made with margarine, but much more common nowadays are spiffy bakeries that invest in interior design and develop a carefully curated range of offerings. Gontran Cherrier is among the most talented to have adopted this approach.

His first bakery, in a residential part of the 18th arrondissement, is a bright and high-ceilinged space that sells beautiful specialty breads and delicate pastries. I have a weakness for his rye and red miso bread, an imposing loaf, dark and volcanic-looking with a robust crust. The flavor is unlike that of any bread I've ever tasted, the malty aromas of rye joining forces with the umami tang of red miso (also called *aka* miso).

I was able to gather some intel on Cherrier's recipe (*merci, Gontran!*) and this home version is close to the original. The two-step, *pâte fermentée* technique creates complex flavor without requiring a sourdough starter. You'll find the dense, cake-like crumb particularly swoonworthy with butter, nut butter, or cheese.

FOR THE FERMENTED DOUGH

½ teaspoon active dry yeast

½ cup (120 ml) lukewarm water

4½ ounces (130 g) rye flour (about 1 cup)

½ teaspoon fine sea salt

FOR THE FINAL DOUGH

½ teaspoon active dry yeast

¾ cup (180 ml) lukewarm water

7 ounces (200 g) rye flour (about 1½ cups), plus more for dusting

2 tablespoons (30 g) red miso

MAKE THE FERMENTED DOUGH AT LEAST THE NIGHT BEFORE SERVING: Proof the yeast in the ½ cup lukewarm water (see How to Proof Yeast, page 21).

In a medium bowl, combine the 4½ ounces (130 g) rye flour, salt, and yeast mixture. Mix with a wooden spoon until the dough comes together in a shaggy ball. Cover the bowl with plastic wrap and let stand at room temperature for 1 to 2 hours. Refrigerate overnight.

Remove the fermented dough from the refrigerator 1 hour before proceeding.

MAKE THE FINAL DOUGH: Proof the yeast in the ¾ cup lukewarm water.

Line a baking sheet with parchment paper. To the fermented dough, add the 7 ounces (200 g) rye flour, the yeast mixture, and the miso. Mix with a wooden spoon until well blended. The dough will be loose and sticky.

(recipe continues)

Scrape onto the baking sheet and use a spatula to shape it into a round loaf shape about 6 inches (15 cm) in diameter. Score the top in parallel grooves with a knife. Dust with a little rye flour, cover loosely with plastic wrap, and let rest for 2 hours at room temperature in a draft-free corner of the kitchen. As it is 100 percent rye, this loaf won't rise dramatically, only about 1½ times its original size.

Put a medium baking dish on the lowest rack of the oven and fill it with about 2 cups (480 ml) boiling water. If you have a pizza stone, put it on the middle rack of the oven.

Preheat the oven to 450°F (230°C).

Uncover the dough. Put the baking sheet in the middle of the oven or, if using a pizza stone, slide the parchment paper carefully onto it, preferably using a pizza peel. Bake for 20 minutes, then reduce the oven temperature to 400°F (200°C), and bake until the loaf is dark brown and sounds hollow when tapped on the bottom, about 30 minutes more.

Transfer to a rack and cool completely before slicing. (If you taste the bread before it's completely cooled, you'll find it gummy and unconvincing. It will improve even further overnight.) Don't expect an airy, open crumb; this is a tight-crumbed bread by design.

IMAGINE FRENCH TOAST AND ALMOND CROISSANT HAVING A BABY TOGETHER. That's what *bostock* is: an ingenious way to upcycle day-old brioche by slathering it with almond cream and baking it again. Topped with slivered almonds and powdered sugar, it makes for a blissful breakfast.

Though it is an old French classic, bostock was only recently brought back into the spotlight, appearing here and there in the display cases of pâtisseries, such as Café Pouchkine, a plush pastry shop and tea salon that is the Paris outpost of a popular Moscow institution. In their rendition, a spoonful of blueberry marmaladè hides between the brioche and the *crème d'amande*, like a surprise pocket of fruity tartness. I am fond of blackberry jam in its place.

FOR THE FILLING AND SYRUP

½ cup (120 ml) Quick Blackberry Jam (recipe follows), or store-bought blackberry or blueberry jam

2 tablespoons sugar

1 tablespoon dark rum (optional)

FOR THE ALMOND CREAM

1 cup (100 g) almond flour

½ cup (100 g) granulated sugar

½ teaspoon fine sea salt

7 tablespoons (100 g) unsalted butter, diced, at room temperature

¼ teaspoon almond extract

2 large eggs

FOR THE BOSTOCK

8 slices day-old brioche loaf or challah (1 inch/2.5 cm thick), or 4 Morning Brioche buns (page 26), split in two (about 12 ounces/340 g total)

½ cup (50 g) sliced almonds

Powdered sugar

· NOTE ·

The syrup and almond cream can be prepared up to 2 days ahead and refrigerated in separate covered containers. Remove from the fridge 1 hour before using.

MAKE THE JAM FILLING: On a tray lined with parchment paper, scoop 8 individual tablespoons of the jam, keeping each one separate but spreading each one slightly into a 2-inch (5 cm) round of jam. Put in the freezer to set for at least 1 hour. These will be slipped between the brioche and the almond cream, and we are freezing them so it's easy to spread the almond cream on top without smudging.

PREPARE THE SYRUP: In a saucepan, combine 240 ml (1 cup) water, the granulated sugar, and rum (if using). Bring to a simmer over medium heat, and cook for 1 minute, stirring to dissolve. Remove from the heat and let the syrup cool. It will be thin.

PREPARE THE ALMOND CREAM: In a stand mixer or food processor, mix the almond flour, granulated sugar, salt, and butter until well blended. Add the almond extract and then the eggs, one by one, and process until creamy. (You can also mix the almond cream by hand, with a spatula.)

Preheat the oven to 350°F (175°C) and line a baking sheet with parchment paper.

(recipe continues)

ASSEMBLE THE BOSTOCKS: Dip the brioche slices in the syrup briefly on both sides and arrange on the baking sheet. Put 1 disk of jam in the center of each slice. Top each with 3 tablespoons almond cream and spread over the entire slice, masking the jam underneath. Sprinkle with 1 tablespoon sliced almonds.

Bake until set and golden brown, 18 to 20 minutes.

Transfer to a rack and sprinkle with powdered sugar. Serve slightly warm or at room temperature.

QUICK BLACKBERRY JAM

Confiture de mûres minute

MAKES ABOUT 1 CUP (240 ML)

BERRIES ARE A LUXURY ITEM IN PARIS; you have to part with quite a bit of cash for a puny little basket that you must eat posthaste, lest the bottom berries spoil before you get to them.

This is what makes foraging for berries so exciting (free fruit!). Ever since I was a young girl, my parents have driven us every September to the Saint-Germain Forest, just outside the city, where blackberry bushes abound along dusty trails. Our loot gets used in tarts, crumbles, fruit salads, and this instant jam, which I sweeten moderately so the flavor of the fruit comes through loud and clear; chia seeds help the jam set.

7 ounces (200 g) blackberries, strawberries, or blueberries (thawed if frozen)

2 tablespoons chia seeds

3 tablespoons honey, rice syrup or agave syrup, plus more to taste

1 teaspoon freshly squeezed lemon juice

Pinch of fine sea salt

Have ready a clean 1-cup (240 ml) glass jar with a lid.

In a blender, combine the berries, chia seeds, honey, lemon juice, and salt and process for a few seconds, until puréed. The mixture should retain some texture.

Transfer to a small saucepan. Bring to a simmer over medium heat and cook, stirring constantly, until the jam thickens and comes together as a springy mass in the pan, about 3 minutes. Spread a teaspoonful on a plate to cool faster, taste, and add a little more honey as needed.

Pour into the jar and close the lid. Cool to room temperature and refrigerate. It will set further in the fridge. Use within 1 week.

FOR A LONG CHAPTER OF MY CHILDHOOD, MY MORNINGS WERE FUELED BY *tartines* of white bread thickly smeared with the famous hazelnut and chocolate spread. I was not alone in this: The rounded glass jar has been a fixture of French breakfasts for decades—with or without the excuse of children in the household.

As a grown-up, and the mother of two young boys now, I look at the ingredient list and put the jar right back on the shelf. But I am still drawn to the magical pairing of hazelnut and chocolate so I make my own version instead: roasted hazelnut butter flavored with cocoa powder and sweetened with dates. This homemade, all-natural "Notella" is not as oily smooth as its factory-made counterpart; I find that finely nubby texture even more enjoyable, whether spread on brioche or rolled up in a Buckwheat Crêpe (page 81).

~NOTELLA~

CHOCOLATE
HAZELNUT
SPREAD

**MAKES ABOUT 1 CUP
(240 ML)**

2 cups (260 g) roasted and skinned hazelnuts (see How to Roast and Skin Hazelnuts, below)

2 tablespoons unsweetened Dutch-process cocoa powder, or more to taste

4 Medjool dates, pitted and chopped, or more to taste

¼ teaspoon fine sea salt

In a food processor or blender, process the hazelnuts until they release their oil and turn into hazelnut butter. At first, it will seem like nothing's happening, but suddenly everything will start to come together. Stop to scrape down the sides from time to time as needed. The mixture will be creamy, with still a little texture to it. Depending on how powerful your appliance is, this will take anywhere from 1 to 4 minutes. If you have an entry-level model, stop more frequently to let the motor cool.

Add the cocoa powder, dates, and salt and process again until fully incorporated. Taste and add a little more cocoa powder or chopped dates to adjust the chocolatiness and sweetness to taste.

Transfer to a jar with a tight-fitting lid. You can choose to refrigerate or keep at room temperature, as you do with your nut butters. Eat within a couple of weeks.

 HOW TO ROAST AND SKIN HAZELNUTS

You will find roasted and skinned hazelnuts at most natural foods stores, or you can buy raw hazelnuts and undertake the process yourself. Spread on a rimmed baking sheet and roast in a 350°F (175°C) preheated oven, stirring every 5 minutes, for 12 to 15 minutes. The nuts are ready when their skins begin to split. Drape a clean kitchen towel in a salad bowl and pour in the nuts. Gather the towel into a bundle and rub the nuts vigorously between your hands to loosen the skins. Scoop the hazelnuts out, leaving the skin fragments behind.

LE MARCHÉ

HISTORICALLY, PARIS WAS A FERTILE LAND WHERE ALL SORTS OF vegetables, roots, greens, and grapes were grown. And although the city's growth pushed the fields farther away, Parisians didn't lose their taste for fresh, local produce.

This explains the record number of greenmarkets the city offers (eighty!), serving every neighborhood. Most are open-air (*marchés volants*) and operate two or three half days a week; a handful are indoor markets (*marchés couverts*) open every day. Whether or not you have errands to run, it is always refreshing to walk through these markets, admiring the displays and dreaming about future meals.

My favorites are the all-organic farmers' market on boulevard des Batignolles, the market on place Monge, and the Marché du Président Wilson. (Find a full list of locations and days at cnz.to/paris-markets.)

In addition, every neighborhood in Paris centers on a bustling market street (*rue commerçante*) that offers a high concentration of specialized food shops: bakeries, butcher shops, fish stalls, cheese shops, charcuteries, wine shops, delis, pastry and chocolate shops, tea and spice shops . . . Parisians conduct their food shopping at a leisurely pace on weekend mornings, walking from shop to shop, chatting with favorite vendors, bumping into neighbors, and sitting down at café terraces to take a break.

Some of my favorite shopping streets are rue des Martyrs, rue des Abbesses, rue Lepic, rue Cler, rue des Rosiers, rue Montorgueil, rue du Faubourg-Saint-Denis, rue Daguerre, and rue Poncelet.

NOON

LE MIDI

La Seine qui se promène
Et me guide du doigt
Et c'est Paris toujours
—JACQUES BREL

THE FRENCH ARE FAMOUS FOR THEIR LONG (VERY LONG) lunch breaks.

This habit, I'm sorry to say, is going the way of the beret; studies show the midday respite shrinks every year as the modern workplace becomes more pressured. What hasn't changed, however, is the idea that the lunch break is for socializing and for pleasure.

In Paris, this means meeting a friend at a nearby bistro, taking advantage of the *plat du jour* (day's special), quickly served and moderately priced. Or going out with coworkers to pick up something from one of the many take-out spots that cater to the office crowd with healthful options inspired by regional *terroir* flavors, or street foods from around the world. Or simply gathering in the office kitchen and popping open packed lunches.

This focus on good people and good food extends well into the weekend when, in spite of full schedules and long lists of errands, Parisians make time for special lunches. They plop their children on the leather banquettes of a favorite brasserie, or host friends for a casual back-from-the-market lunch, or go back to their parents' for a full-on Sunday lunch of roast chicken.

You'll find a bit of all those things here, with the tried-and-true recipes Parisians use to wow their friends and their *bonne-maman*.

THIS OMELET IS ON THE MENU AT LAZARE, THE CLASSIC FRENCH RESTAURANT
that Michelin-starred chef Éric Frechon runs within Paris's Saint-Lazare
train station. As is the fashion in modern brasseries, Lazare features a
semainier, a roster of seven dishes each available one day a week—a clever
way to build anticipation, as well as encourage customers to come back
again and again, until their collection is complete. Thursday is *lapin à la
casserole* (braised rabbit), Friday is *brandade de morue* (salt cod gratin),
and come Saturday, the kitchen is ready to roll out potato chip omelets to
eager diners and their offspring.

I imagine I don't have to sell you too hard on the idea of this dish. (I
had you at "potato chip," right?) It's an easy one to make at home, and the
perfect use for the crushed bits of chips at the bottom of the bag. (A recipe
tester who shall remain anonymous said it was excellent hangover food.)

~OMELETTE~
aux chips et ciboulette

POTATO CHIP & CHIVE OMELET

SERVES 2

4 large eggs

About 1 cup somewhat
crushed salted potato chips
(2½ ounces/70 g)

3 tablespoons finely chopped
fresh chives

1 teaspoon dried garlic flakes

1 teaspoon unsalted butter
or olive oil

Salad greens lightly dressed with
Bistro Vinaigrette (page 54),
for serving

· NOTES ·

This recipe halves easily.

This works best with thicker chips,
and you can play around with
different flavors.

No salt is added to the eggs, as
potato chips are typically salty.
Adjust the seasoning if you are
using low-salt chips.

In a medium bowl, beat the eggs lightly with a fork.

In a second bowl, combine the potato chips, chives, and garlic flakes.
Stir half into the eggs.

In a medium skillet, melt the butter over medium heat. When it foams,
add the eggs. Cook the eggs for 2 minutes, then sprinkle the remaining
chips over the surface. Cook for 1 more minute, or until the omelet is
cooked to your taste. I like mine *baveuse*: still a little runny in the middle.

Fold the omelet in two and slide onto a serving plate. Serve immediately,
before the chips lose their crunch, with a side of salad greens.

~SALADE~
de courgettes spiralisées
à la pêche et aux amandes
fraîches

SPIRALIZED ZUCCHINI SALAD
WITH PEACH & GREEN ALMONDS

SERVES 4

WALK PAST THE SIDEWALK DISPLAY OF A PRODUCE SHOP IN PARIS IN THE summer, and you may look quizzically at the soft green pods labeled *amandes fraîches*. Pastel green and fuzzy like a peach, they are a prized item for cooks in the know, who will have the vendor fill up a paper bag and carry it home with a private glow on their face.

Armed with a sharp knife, they will slice through the thick outer skins to reveal the immature almonds inside, ivory white and glossy. More tender than dried almonds and milkier in taste, they can be enjoyed as a lovely snack right then and there, standing at the counter, or sprinkled over salads for flavor and snap.

If you find green almonds, add them to this salad of zucchini "noodles" sweetened by sliced yellow peaches, a quick and nutritious height-of-the-summer appetizer that can also serve as a side, with grilled fish or chicken. If green almonds are not available, soak dried almonds overnight and pat dry.

· NOTES ·

Use fresh zucchini that feel firm from one end to the other.

To make this ahead of time, toss all the ingredients together but hold the salt until the last minute, or the moisture drawn out of the zucchini will make the salad soupy.

3 medium zucchini (about 1¼ pounds/550 g total)

2 tablespoons olive oil

1 tablespoon freshly squeezed lemon juice

¾ teaspoon fine sea salt

¼ teaspoon finely chopped rosemary, fresh or dried

1 peach (about 6 ounces/170 g), peeled and sliced

20 green almonds, peeled

Freshly ground black pepper

Cut the zucchini into thin noodles using a spiralizer or julienne slicer. Put in a medium salad bowl and give the noodles a few snips with kitchen scissors for easier eating. Add the olive oil, lemon juice, salt, and rosemary and toss to coat. Taste and adjust the seasoning.

Divide the zucchini among 4 plates. Top with the peach slices and almonds. Sprinkle with black pepper and serve.

WHILE MANY OLD-SCHOOL BRASSERIES AND CORNER BISTROS STILL HAVE menus heavily weighted toward meat and seafood, vegetarians can always count on finding a roasted goat cheese salad on the menu. Lucky for them, it's usually delicious, and a favorite of many cheese-loving omnivores, too: thick rounds of goat cheese, breaded and seasoned, placed on pieces of bread, grilled under the broiler, and served bubbling hot on a bed of dressed greens.

Hazelnut crumbs and dried herbs in place of the usual bread crumbs update this classic, as do apple slices instead of toasts. They create a refreshing twist that is also gluten-free; a recipe tester for this book called it one of the best salads she and her husband had ever eaten.

~SALADE~
de chèvre en panure de noisette et pomme

HAZELNUT-CRUSTED GOAT CHEESE & APPLE SALAD

SERVES 4

Olive oil

½ cup (60 g) hazelnuts, toasted, skinned (see How to Roast and Skin Hazelnuts, page 43), and finely chopped

4 teaspoons mixed dried herbs, such as herbes de Provence

2 teaspoons dried garlic flakes

¼ teaspoon fine sea salt

4 crisp apples, preferably small (4 to 6 ounces/120 to 170 g each)

9 ounces (250 g) fresh goat cheese, crottin or log

8 cups (160 g) loosely packed mixed greens

¼ cup (60 ml) Bistro Vinaigrette (recipe follows)

Fresh chervil or flat-leaf parsley, roughly chopped

Freshly ground black pepper

Preheat the oven to 400°F (200°C). Lightly grease a baking sheet with olive oil.

In a shallow bowl, combine the hazelnuts, herbs, garlic, and salt.

Core the apples and slice horizontally at their widest to get a total of 12 round slices about ½ inch (1.25 cm) thick. Press the apple slices into the hazelnut mixture to coat on each side, and put on the baking sheet.

Slice the goat cheese to get 12 rounds about ½ inch (1.25 cm) thick. Dip each round in the hazelnut mix, turning and pressing delicately to coat all sides. Put a goat cheese round on top of each apple slice.

Bake the apple-cheese stacks until the cheese is bubbling, 8 to 10 minutes.

Dress the mixed greens with the vinaigrette and divide among 4 salad bowls.

Arrange 3 apple and goat cheese slices over each bowl of greens, sprinkle with chervil and pepper, and serve.

· **VARIATION** ·
In summer, replace the apple slices with halved peaches or nectarines.

(recipe continues)

BISTRO VINAIGRETTE

La vinaigrette des bistros

MAKES ABOUT
²/₃ CUP
(160 ML);
1 TABLESPOON
DRESSES
2 CUPS
OF GREENS

MANY FOREIGNERS RECOUNT, with moist eyes, the epiphany they experienced upon tasting their first green salad in Paris. Such vivacity, such zest in these few forkfuls of green! It has to do with the freshness of the lettuce, but the real secret lies in the dressing, a deceptively simple combination of mustard, vinegar, and oil that coats greens with a silky film and complements their flavor without obliterating it.

Making vinaigrette is a skill acquired early in France. Most cooks just whisk it right in the salad bowl, without measuring, until the consistency is the right shade of creamy, dipping the tip of a finger to taste and adjust. This, however, is my recipe.

Use good wine vinegar—red or white—and strong Dijon mustard. But the real kicker is the oil: Tempted as you are to use your best olive oil, it is too assertive; the classic French vinaigrette is made with a milder oil, such as sunflower seed or grapeseed. Also key is the layer of flavor provided by the shallot.

A final word of advice (almost done, I promise): Dry your greens carefully so the dressing will cling to them. I do as my mother has done for decades: After taking the leaves out of the salad spinner, I roll them in a clean kitchen towel to absorb extra moisture. You can put this bundle straight in the fridge; it keeps for up to a day.

· VARIATIONS ·

Substitute other vinegars or lemon juice for the wine vinegar.

Add 1 teaspoon honey along with the mustard.

Before adding the oil, stir in 1 tablespoon crème fraîche (or sour cream) for brightness.

Substitute a more assertive oil, such as olive, hazelnut, or walnut oil, for one-third of the neutral oil (e.g., 2 tablespoons walnut oil to 4 tablespoons grapeseed oil).

Add finely snipped fresh herbs, especially flat-leaf parsley, chives, or chervil, along with the salad greens.

1 tablespoon finely diced shallot

½ teaspoon fine sea salt

2 tablespoons wine vinegar, red or white

1 tablespoon Dijon mustard

6 tablespoons neutral oil, such as sunflower seed, grapeseed, or canola

Freshly ground pepper (white if available)

In a medium bowl, combine the shallot, salt, and vinegar with a wooden spoon. Let rest for 10 minutes to take the edge off the shallot.

Stir in the mustard. Pour in the oil slowly, stirring all the while to create an emulsion. Sprinkle generously with pepper. Taste and adjust the seasoning. The dressing can be prepared a few hours ahead. Cover and refrigerate until ready to serve. Leftover vinaigrette keeps for up to 1 week in the fridge, in a glass jar with a tight lid.

THIS SIMPLE CARPACCIO OF SHAVED AUTUMN VEGETABLES IS ONE OF MY favorite back-from-the-*marché* recipes. It is inspired by a dish at Jeanne B., a Montmartre restaurant that serves a home-style cuisine focusing on seasonal ingredients and rotisserie meats. The paper-thin vegetables, seasoned with a tangy dressing and topped with herbs and chopped hazelnuts, bring a brightness and crunch to the table that are unexpected that time of year. I add black tapenade (olive paste) for extra oomph. Any combination of seasonal crudités works here; this quartet of carrots, mushrooms, cauliflower, and beets is beautiful in color, texture, and flavor.

1 medium carrot, about 4 ounces (115 g), peeled

1 cup (85 g) button mushrooms, trimmed

½ cup (115 g) cauliflower florets

½ medium beet, about 4 ounces (115 g), peeled

¼ cup (60 ml) freshly squeezed lemon juice

¼ cup (60 ml) olive oil

Fine sea salt and freshly ground black pepper

3 tablespoons finely chopped fresh chives or cilantro

½ cup (50 g) hazelnuts, roasted and skinned (see How to Roast and Skin Hazelnuts, page 43), roughly chopped

2 tablespoons store-bought black olive tapenade

Using a mandoline, slice the carrots, mushrooms, cauliflower, and beet into paper-thin shavings, reserving them separately as you go. (The cauliflower will crumble; that's fine.)

In a bowl, whisk together the lemon juice and olive oil.

Arrange the sliced vegetables in a scattered stack in the center of 6 appetizer plates, alternating vegetables for an attractive contrast of colors. This is not meant to be a neat stack; don't overthink it. Drizzle each stack with 1 tablespoon of the dressing. Sprinkle with salt, pepper, chives, and hazelnuts.

Whisk the tapenade into the remaining dressing, spoon on the side of each plate, and serve.

GRATED CARROTS

FROM THE CHARCUTERIE

SERVES 4 TO 6

EVERY MARKET STREET IN PARIS BOASTS ONE OR TWO CHARCUTERIES primarily focused on whole-hog products, such as dried sausages, hams, and pâtés: That's what the word *charcuterie* encompasses. These shops are also providers of classic French dishes, freshly made and ready for you to take home and feast on. This spans the entire old-school repertoire, from *bouchées à la reine* to *lapin chasseur* and *œufs en neige*. I love to step into my neighborhood charcuterie to admire the gilded serving dishes, the gleam of aspic, and the frilly tufts of parsley. For a reasonable price, it is easy to put together a varied and balanced meal from the offerings *du jour*.

That said, one of my favorite items is one easily made at home: *carottes râpées*, a classic of the French roster of hors d'oeuvres that is a study in simplicity. If you use fresh and juicy carrots, which abound in Paris market stalls in the spring, you don't need much to turn them into the freshest, sweetest, tangiest of salads. It is also an ideal canvas for various vinegars and oils and additions, so I've included a cheat sheet of variations if you want to run away with the concept.

· NOTES ·

Young carrots with a thin, smooth skin may not require peeling. Taste a thin slice of carrot with the skin on: If there is no bitterness, skip the peeling.

The utensil you use to grate the carrots, and the size and thickness of the carrot strands it produces, will yield very different results in terms of texture; the thicker the strands, the crunchier the salad.

4 medium carrots (1 pound/450 g), peeled (see Notes)

1 tablespoon sherry vinegar or red wine vinegar

¾ teaspoon fine sea salt

3 tablespoons neutral oil, such as sunflower seed, grapeseed, or canola

Freshly ground black pepper

Using a box grater, the grater attachment of your food processor, or a mandoline with the comb attachment, grate the carrots (see Notes). This should yield about 3½ cups grated carrots.

In a salad bowl, stir together the vinegar and salt until the salt is dissolved. Whisk in the oil. Add the carrots and stir well. Sprinkle with black pepper. Taste and adjust the seasoning.

You can serve the salad immediately, or reserve in the refrigerator, covered, for up to 8 hours. Stir again before serving.

≡ OPTIONAL ADD-ONS ≡
(Choose 2 or 3)

ADD TO THE SALT AND VINEGAR

- Fresh garlic, finely chopped
- Shallot, finely diced
- Ground cumin, coriander, or ginger
- Dijon mustard
- Anchovies in brine, drained and minced
- A pinch of sugar, especially if you're dealing with older, less sweet carrots
- A drop of orange blossom water

USE IN PLACE OF THE VINEGAR

- Lemon juice, freshly squeezed, and lemon zest
- Orange juice, freshly squeezed, and orange zest

REPLACE ONE-THIRD OF THE OIL WITH:

- Walnut oil, hazelnut oil, or sesame oil

ADD ALONG WITH THE CARROTS

- Grated beets, fennel, or apple
- Diced avocado

FOLD IN AT THE END

- Raisins
- Sunflower seeds, pumpkin seeds, pistachios, poppy seeds, walnuts, sesame seeds
- Chopped fresh herbs, especially chives, flat-leaf parsley, cilantro, dill, or chervil
- Preserved lemon, finely diced
- Black or green olives, halved or chopped
- Hard-boiled eggs (page 62), chopped

WHEN YOU STOP FOR LUNCH AT A TYPICAL PARIS CAFÉ, YOU ARE HANDED a tall laminated menu listing your options, including *salades-repas*, or meal-size salads. Before ordering one, I cast sideways glances at other peoples' plates, peek through to the kitchen on my way to the bathroom, and try to assess just how fresh everything is. This determines whether I choose a salad, opt for more of a sure thing such as a Croque-Madame (page 69), or in the extreme, flee the scene.

When my detective work has green-lighted the salads, I love a good *frisée aux lardons*, a classic combo of wispy, curly lettuce strands that have a slight bitterness to them, like dandelion greens or escarole, tempered by the salty chew of bacon strips, the soothing velvet of eggs, and the toasted crunch of croutons. In the classic version, the eggs are poached, so the runny yolk will further dress the greens—if you'd like to do that, follow the poaching directions in Poached Eggs with Bread Crumbs and Onion Pickle (page 17). An easier alternative is to make steamed hard-boiled eggs, undercooking them slightly so the white is set but the yolk is creamy.

~FRISÉE~
aux lardons et aux œufs

FRISÉE
WITH BACON & EGG

SERVES 4 AS AN APPETIZER OR 2 AS A MAIN COURSE

5 slices (about 5 ounces/150 g) thick-cut bacon, cut into short, thin strips to make lardons (see Note)

8 cups (160 g) frisée lettuce (also called chicory or curly endive), dandelion greens, or chopped escarole

¼ cup Bistro Vinaigrette (page 54)

4 Steamed Hard-Boiled Eggs (recipe follows), shelled and halved

½ recipe Quick Croutons (recipe follows)

2 tablespoons chopped fresh chives

· NOTE ·

French cooks typically use bacon in the form of *lardons*, short and thin strips of pork belly, which they purchase presliced and ready to cook. To make your own, get thick-cut bacon and slice it across the grain into short matchsticks.

In a dry skillet over medium heat, cook the bacon, stirring frequently, until browned, about 5 minutes. Scoop into a bowl. (Keep the rendered fat for another use.)

In a large salad bowl, dress the frisée with the vinaigrette.

Divide the frisée among salad plates, forming nests. Top with the halved eggs and sprinkle with the bacon strips, croutons, and chives.

(recipe continues)

STEAMED HARD-BOILED EGGS

Œufs durs à la vapeur

MAKES 6

HARD-BOILED EGGS should be the simplest thing in the world, but they are a finicky thing to master. It's not just about avoiding the dreaded ring of gray around the yolk. It's also about getting the texture right—and about the peeling, and how maddening it is when the shell clings to the white, leaving you with a mangled egg, and a sudden urge to cry. Steaming eggs is the answer: It's easy and the eggs are a dream to peel.

6 large eggs

Set up a steamer, bringing the water to a boil. Prepare an ice bath by placing a dozen ice cubes in a medium bowl and filling it with cold water.

Put the eggs in the steamer basket, cover, and steam for 7 to 12 minutes, depending on how you want your eggs—soft-boiled to hard-boiled. (It may take you a couple of tries to get the timing exactly right for your taste; make a note of it.)

Transfer the eggs to the ice bath using a slotted spoon or tongs to cool completely.

To peel, tap each egg gently on the counter to crack the shell all over, then peel it off. Unpeeled hard-boiled eggs will keep for up to 5 days in the fridge.

QUICK CROUTONS

Croûtons rapides

MAKES 2 CUPS
(100 G)

WHEN YOU'VE GONE TO THE TROUBLE of buying good artisanal bread—say, a loaf of sourdough or a French-style baguette—it can be heartbreaking to see the leftovers go dry or chewy. When that happens, you're only two steps away from golden croutons: Just dice and sauté the bread in a little butter. They can be kept for a few days on the counter, and thrown by the handful into salads and soups.

· **NOTE** ·
I aim for ⅓-inch (1 cm) cubes and use a bread knife.

2 teaspoons unsalted butter

2 cups (110 g) cubed day-old sourdough bread or baguette (see Note)

¼ teaspoon fine sea salt

In a small skillet, melt the butter over medium heat. When it foams, add the bread and salt. Cook, stirring frequently, until golden, 3 to 5 minutes.

The croutons will crisp up as they cool.

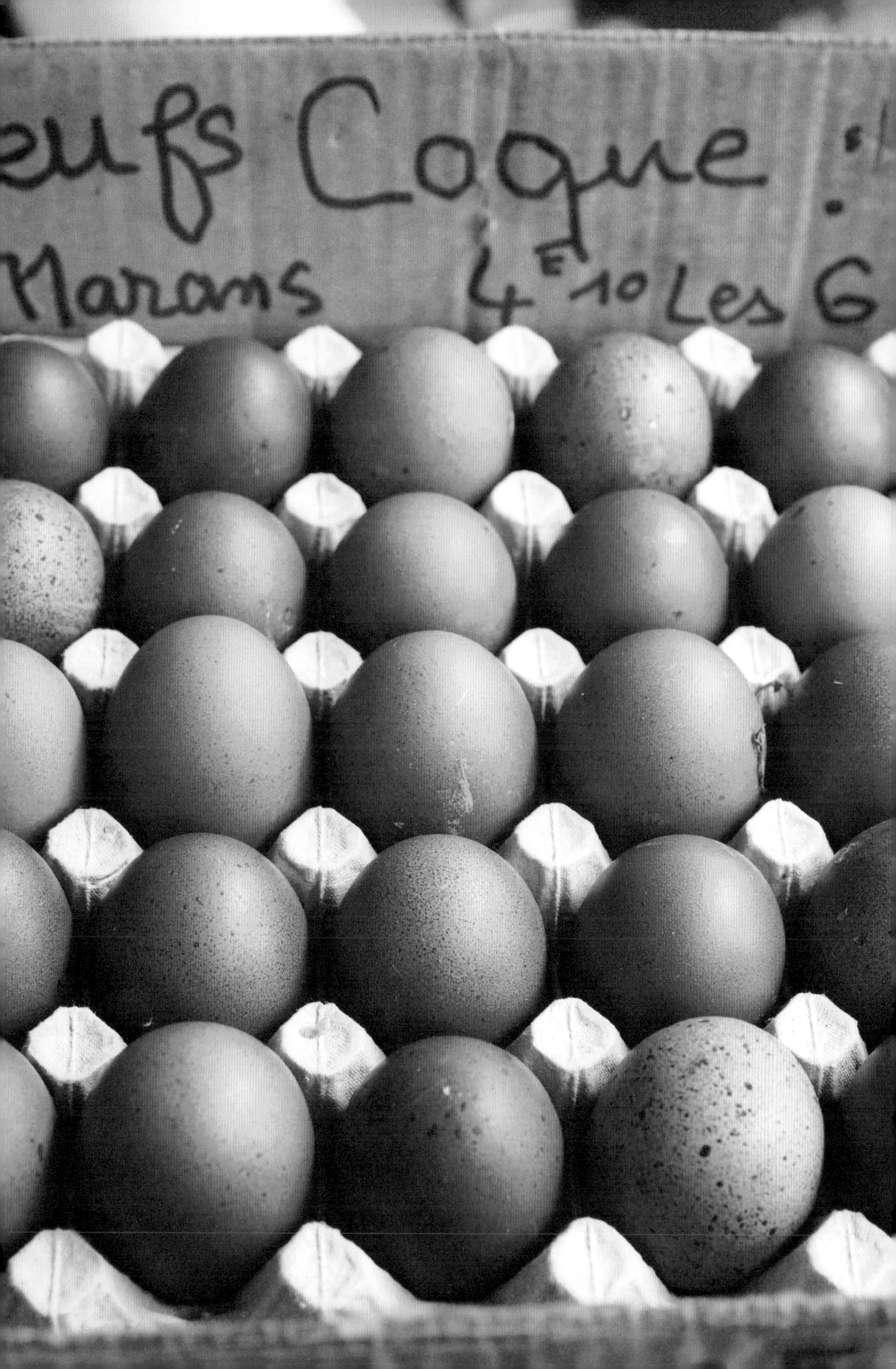
eufs Coque
Marans 4€10 Les 6

~SOUPE DE LENTILLES~
saucisse et fenouil

LENTIL SOUP
WITH SAUSAGE & FENNEL

SERVES 6

THE FRENCH PRIZE LENTILS THAT HOLD THEIR SHAPE IN COOKING. The most famous is probably the *lentille verte du Puy* from Auvergne, protected by an appellation of origin. I am also very fond of the *lentille blonde de Saint-Flour* from the same region, which was saved from oblivion in the nineties, and recognized by the Slow Food movement. The tiny, light-brown lentil cooks into sweet little nibs that pop under tooth in the most delicate way. This makes it perfect for zesty, filling salads dressed with Bistro Vinaigrette (page 54), but it works just as well in soups, which appear on Paris bistro menus during the chillier months. I adore this recipe, cooked with diced fennel and chunks of Toulouse sausage. It comes together easily and improves overnight.

1½ cups (300 g) green or brown lentils, preferably French

1 teaspoon baking soda

7 ounces (200 g) Toulouse sausage, or other uncooked pork sausage, casings removed

Olive oil, as needed

1 medium yellow onion, diced

1 medium bulb fennel, trimmed, cored, and diced (or substitute 4 celery stalks)

½ teaspoon fine sea salt

3 whole cloves

½ teaspoon dried thyme

6 cups (1.5 liters) chicken or vegetable stock

Freshly ground black pepper

Crème fraîche or full-fat sour cream, for serving

Roughly chopped fresh flat-leaf parsley, for serving

Hot sauce, for serving (optional)

The day before you want to cook them, soak the lentils in enough cold water to cover by 2 inches (5 cm) mixed with the baking soda.

The next day, in a heavy-bottomed pot, cook the sausage over medium heat until browned, breaking it into bits with a wooden spoon as it cooks. (If the sausage meat is lean, add 2 teaspoons olive oil so it doesn't stick.) Scoop out and set aside on a plate.

Add the onion, fennel, and salt to the pot and cook, stirring regularly, until softened, 4 to 5 minutes.

Drain and rinse the lentils. Add to the pot with the cloves and thyme. Add the stock, cover, and bring to a simmer. Cook until the lentils are cooked through, 35 to 40 minutes. If you want to give more body to the soup, mash roughly with a potato masher, or process briefly with an immersion blender. You want the soup to remain chunky.

Return the sausage to the pot and stir. Taste and adjust the seasoning.

Ladle into bowls. Add a spoonful of crème fraîche, black pepper, and parsley, and serve. I like a dash of hot sauce, too.

THE
BEST BAGUETTE
IN PARIS

EVERY YEAR IN MARCH, BREAD LOVERS HOLD THEIR BREATH AS AN ALL-important competition takes place to select the Meilleure Baguette de Paris. It is organized by the mayor's office with the purpose of encouraging bakers to improve their craft and publicizing the truly exceptional talents the city houses.

Any baker can enter. The baguettes are tasted and evaluated anonymously by a jury made up of bakers, chefs, journalists, and ordinary citizens, who can put their name in and hope to be selected. Each baguette is rated for appearance, smell, texture, and flavor; and at the end of the day, the top-ranking ones are announced.

The winning bakery gets a publicity boost in the press, and bread enthusiasts will travel across the city to taste the new best baguette. The winner also receives a few thousand euros, and the privilege of providing baguettes for the Élysée, the French presidential palace, where official meals are held for foreign heads of state and diplomats.

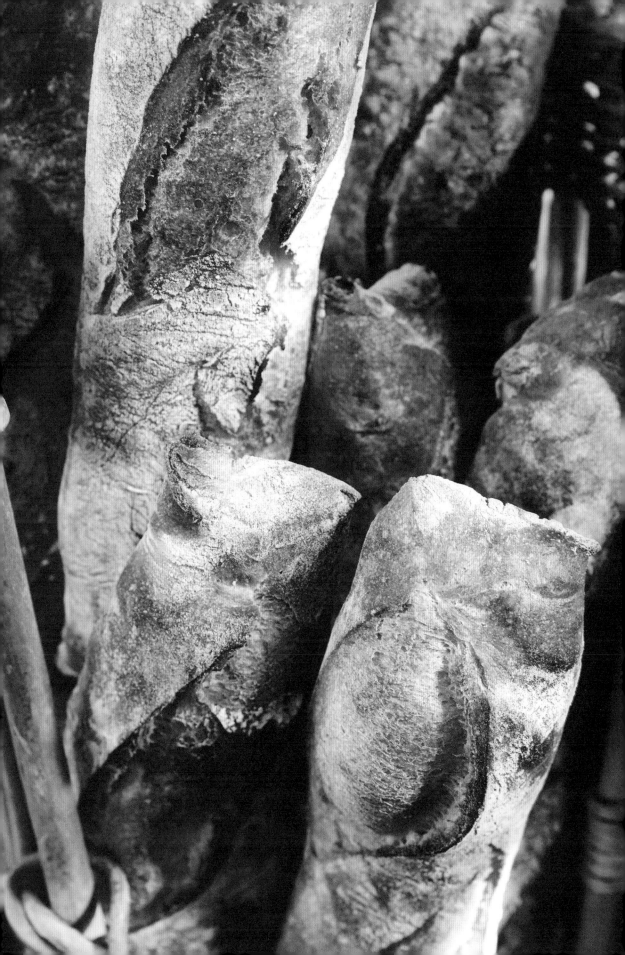

WHEN MY HUSBAND AND I STARTED DATING, AT THE TENDER AGE OF seventeen, we were freshmen at the same university in Paris and spent much of our free time sitting close together in cafés in the neighborhood. When lunchtime rolled around, if we were feeling flush, we would treat ourselves to the best-value item on the menu: the *croque-madame*, a grilled sandwich of ham and cheese topped with a fried egg, served with a salad. (Hold the egg and you've got a *croque-monsieur*.)

When served at a Paris bistro, it is rich with béchamel sauce and a thick mantle of melted cheese. This is perfect for hungry students. The version we make at home now, twenty years later, skips the béchamel and uses just enough cheese to make the insides divinely gooey yet preserve the crispness of the bread.

~CROQUE-MADAME~

GRILLED CHEESE SANDWICH WITH HAM & EGG

SERVES 4

3 tablespoons (40 g) unsalted butter, at room temperature

8 large slices sandwich bread, about ½ inch (1.25 cm) thick

4 teaspoons strong Dijon mustard, plus more for serving

1 cup shaved or grated hard cheese, such as Comté or Gruyère (3½ ounces/100 g)

5 ounces (140 g) thinly sliced ham

2 teaspoons olive oil

4 large eggs

¼ teaspoon fine sea salt

Salad greens dressed lightly with Bistro Vinaigrette (page 54), for serving

· NOTE ·

If you have a panini press, preheat it and cook the sandwiches for 3 to 4 minutes.

Preheat the broiler.

Spread softened butter on just one side of the bread slices and put the bread buttered side down on a cutting board. Spread half of the bread slices on their unbuttered side with the mustard and top with half of the cheese. Layer the ham on top, follow with the remaining cheese, and top with a bread slice, buttered side up.

Put the sandwiches on a baking sheet and broil for 4 minutes. Press with a spatula, flip, and broil until golden, another 2 minutes.

Meanwhile, in a large skillet, heat the oil over medium-high heat. Add the eggs, sprinkle with salt, and cook until the whites are set and golden at the edges but the yolks are still runny.

Divide the sandwiches among 4 plates and top each with a fried egg. Serve with salad greens.

~LAHMAJOUN~

TURKISH LAMB
FLATBREADS

**MAKES EIGHT 8-INCH (20 CM)
LAHMAJOUNS; SERVES 6 TO 8**

TO THE HUNTER OF GOOD EATS, THERE ARE FEW THINGS MORE APPEALING than hole-in-the-wall finds. Walking around Paris's Faubourg-Saint-Denis area, I always end up at one of the many Turkish sandwich shacks, drawn in by the guy kneading and rolling out flatbread in the window. The pliable rounds are used to assemble kebab wraps and—my hands-down favorite—*lahmajouns*.

Sometimes described as Kurdish pizza (yet also claimed by Armenians, Syrians, and the Lebanese), lahmajoun is a street food that consists of a mixture of ground meat (beef, lamb, or both) and vegetables (tomatoes, onions, bell pepper) on top of those flatbreads. Once cooked and garnished with lettuce and onion, it is rolled up and eaten with a tall glass of *ayran*, a salty fermented milk.

I love everything about the lahmajoun, including making it at home with friends; both the dough and the filling can be prepared the day before.

FOR THE DOUGH

1½ teaspoons active dry yeast

⅔ cup lukewarm water

1 pound (450 g) all-purpose flour (about 3½ cups), plus more for rolling

½ cup (120 ml) plain whole-milk yogurt

1 tablespoon neutral oil, such as sunflower seed, grapeseed, or canola, plus more for the pan

1 teaspoon sugar

¾ teaspoon fine sea salt

FOR THE TOPPING

10 ounces (280 g) ground beef, lamb, or a mix

½ cup (100 g) seeded and chopped tomato

¼ cup (45 g) finely diced green bell pepper

¼ cup (50 g) finely chopped red onion

¼ cup (15 g) chopped fresh flat-leaf parsley

¼ cup (60 ml) tomato paste

1 garlic clove, finely chopped

1 teaspoon ground cumin

1 teaspoon paprika

¾ teaspoon fine sea salt

¼ teaspoon freshly ground black pepper

FOR BRUSHING

¼ cup (60 ml) tomato paste

¼ cup (60 ml) olive oil

FOR SERVING

1 cup (50 g) finely sliced lettuce

½ cup (100 g) finely sliced red onion

1 lemon, cut into wedges

Hot sauce (optional)

(recipe continues)

Start making the dough 1½ hours ahead, or the day before serving for better flavor: Proof the yeast in the lukewarm water (see How to Proof Yeast, page 21).

In the bowl of a stand mixer fitted with the dough hook, combine the flour, yeast mixture, yogurt, oil, sugar, and salt. Knead on medium speed until the dough is smooth and elastic, about 4 minutes. If the dough seems too dry to come together, add a little more water, 1 tablespoon at a time. (You can also mix and knead the dough by hand on your countertop; it will take about 8 minutes of kneading.)

If preparing the dough a day ahead, scrape into a bowl, cover tightly, and refrigerate. Remove from the fridge 1 hour before using. If making on the same day, cover and let rest for 1 hour at room temperature in a draft-free corner of the kitchen.

MAKE THE TOPPING: In a large bowl, use your hands to mix together the ground meat, tomato, bell pepper, onion, parsley, tomato paste, garlic, cumin, paprika, salt, and black pepper until thoroughly combined. This can be made up to a day ahead. Refrigerate in an airtight container.

Preheat the oven to 425°F (220°F). Grease a large baking sheet with oil.

On a lightly floured work surface with a lightly floured rolling pin, roll the dough out into a long rectangle, then fold it in three like a letter. Give the dough a quarter of a turn, roll into a rectangle again, and fold in three again, adding a light sprinkling of flour as needed to prevent sticking. Repeat once or twice more; the dough will get stiffer as you go.

Divide the dough into 8 equal pieces, about 3⅓ ounces (90 g) each. Roll out two pieces of dough into thin ovals about 8 × 7 inches (20 × 18 cm) and put on the baking sheet; keep the others covered with a kitchen towel.

MAKE THE MIXTURE FOR BRUSHING: In a bowl, whisk together the tomato paste and olive oil. Brush the entire top of each lahmajoun with the mixture (no border), and top each with ¼ cup of the filling, using the tips of your fingers to spread and press into the dough.

Bake until the topping is cooked through and the crust is lightly golden, about 12 minutes. Don't overbake, or they will not be pliable enough to roll up.

Flip one lahmajoun onto the other so they're face-to-face. Transfer to a plate and cover tightly with 2 layers of foil while you bake the others. Stack them on the plate as you go to keep them warm and pliable.

TO SERVE: Garnish each lahmajoun with sliced lettuce, red onion, a squeeze of lemon juice, and some hot sauce, if desired. Roll up and eat.

THE ICONIC PARISIAN SANDWICH IS THE JAMBON-BEURRE, A BAGUETTE sandwich filled with butter and cooked ham. Yet I am partial to the *sandwich tunisien*, a baguette overflowing with the staple salad of Tunisia, cucumber, tomato, bell pepper, onion, and cilantro, plus tuna, diced potatoes, and olives. *Salade niçoise* in a sandwich, if you will. And the *tunisien* at Chez Harry, a Jewish-Tunisian hole-in-the-wall in the Sentier, the former garment district, was my favorite until Harry retired and shuttered it for good. He had been running the shop for decades, closing for Shabbat every Saturday, and feeding a working crowd the rest of the week. He also had a loyal clientele of older guys who spent their days there playing cards (*belote*, to be precise) and pushed their chairs aside in a grumble when you needed to squeeze into a nearby table.

The kitchen staff assembled the sandwich to order, so the ingredients had barely met when you bit in, and you could taste their respective flavors distinctly.

TUNISIAN
SANDWICH

SERVES 4

⅓ medium cucumber, finely diced

1 medium tomato, finely diced

⅓ large red bell pepper, finely diced

¼ medium red onion, finely diced

⅓ cup roughly chopped fresh cilantro leaves

¼ teaspoon fine sea salt, or more to taste

Freshly ground black pepper

5½ ounces (150 g) high-quality canned or jarred tuna in olive oil

1 medium starchy potato, peeled, boiled, and cut into cubes

1 small preserved lemon (pulp and rind), diced

20 black brine- or oil-cured olives, drained and pitted

2 fresh baguettes (about 9 ounces/250 g each)

2 tablespoons harissa, or to taste

· NOTES ·

The amount of filling needed depends on the size and shape of the bread. Don't force the issue if it seems full and you have extra ingredients; serve the leftovers as a salad the next day.

Cut each baguette into 3 pieces if you want 6 smaller sandwiches.

· VARIATION ·

You can also include capers and hard-boiled eggs.

Prepare the salad 2 to 4 hours ahead if possible. In a medium bowl, toss together the cucumber, tomato, bell pepper, onion, cilantro, salt, and some pepper. Drain the tuna, reserving 1 tablespoon of the oil. Toss the oil with the vegetables in the bowl. Taste and adjust the seasoning; you want this slightly undersalted. Cover the salad and refrigerate.

Flake the tuna into a small bowl. Put the remaining fillings—potato, preserved lemon, and olives—in separate small bowls.

Halve each baguette crosswise and then slice each piece in half horizontally. Open each half baguette and remove some of the crumb if needed to make room for the fillings. Spread the bottom half with 1 to 1½ teaspoons harissa, to taste. Scoop in some salad and flaked tuna, and follow with potato cubes, preserved lemon, and olives (see Notes).

Wrap tightly in wax paper for easier eating. Serve immediately, or refrigerate for up to 4 hours. Bring to room temperature before eating.

PARIS PICNIC

IF PICNICKING WERE AN OLYMPIC SPORT, PARISIANS WOULD REAP GOLD;
at the first glimmer of sunshine, they rush outdoors with blankets, cutlery, and a tote of edibles. In the company of like-minded friends, they celebrate the arrival of *les beaux jours* (balmy spring days) and savor the unique sense of freedom that comes from eating out in the open at the heart of a bustling city.

Any bench could do to set up camp, but patches of green, however tiny, are in highest demand, as are spots in close proximity to water: by the river, on footbridges, or along the canals.

Picnic spreads are made up of simple homemade items, such as big salads (like Spiralized Zucchini Salad, page 50, or Frisée with Bacon and Egg, page 61), quiches (see page 85), and quick breads (see Olive and Goat Cheese Quick Bread, page 173). The city's greenmarkets and market streets are teeming with glorious no-cook options as well, from crusty bread and oozy cheese to fine charcuterie and voluptuous pastries.

The most popular spots include the Champ de Mars gardens beneath the Eiffel Tower, the Pont des Arts footbridge, the banks of the Seine (especially the Quai Saint-Bernard, where there is music and dance at night), and the Canal Saint-Martin.

THE POILÂNE BAKERY (SEE PAGE 28) HAS SUCH AN AURA THAT EVERY traditional café in Paris offers *tartines Poilâne*, open-faced sandwiches assembled on long slices of the iconic bread. The best place to get them is straight from the source, at one of Poilâne's bright lunch counters.

To make this one, Apollonia Poilâne's personal favorite, you'll mash smoked fish with herbs into *rillettes* (a lightly chunky pâté) and pair it with a quick-pickled beet relish. It is a simple preparation that has a lot going on: the smoky, salty, sweet, and acidic flavors coming together beautifully with the bread. This can also be offered as bite-size canapés with a predinner drink.

~TARTINE~
de maquereau fumé
au relish de betterave

SMOKED MACKEREL TARTINE WITH BEET RELISH

SERVES 4

FOR THE BEET RELISH

1 large beet (10 ounces/280 g), peeled and grated

2 tablespoons sugar

¼ cup (60 ml) cider vinegar

½ teaspoon ground cumin

½ teaspoon fine sea salt, or more to taste

FOR THE MACKEREL RILLETTES

7 ounces (200 g) smoked mackerel, smoked trout (the flaky kind), or drained canned sardines

¼ cup (60 ml) plain whole-milk yogurt

3 tablespoons finely chopped shallot

2 tablespoons finely chopped fresh chives

1 garlic clove, finely chopped

1 tablespoon freshly squeezed lemon juice

Fine sea salt

FOR SERVING

4 large slices artisanal sourdough bread (ideally Poilâne), about ⅓ inch (1 cm) thick

Freshly ground black pepper

Mixed greens dressed with Bistro Vinaigrette (page 54), for serving

MAKE THE RELISH THE DAY BEFORE SERVING: In a medium saucepan, combine the grated beet, sugar, vinegar, cumin, salt, and ¼ cup (60 ml) water. Bring to a low simmer and cook, stirring from time to time, over medium-low heat until the liquids are absorbed, 15 to 20 minutes. Taste and adjust the seasoning. Cool completely on the counter, then transfer to a container with a tight-fitting lid and refrigerate overnight. Remove from the fridge 1 hour before serving.

MAKE THE RILLETTES THE DAY BEFORE SERVING: Remove the skin from the mackerel using tongs and a fork (the smell of smoked fish is quite persistent on the skin!). In a bowl, shred the fish, removing any obvious bones. Combine with the yogurt, shallot, chives, garlic, and lemon juice to get a chunky pâté. Taste and adjust the seasoning with salt if needed. Cover and refrigerate overnight. Remove from the fridge 1 hour before serving.

TO SERVE: Toast the bread lightly. Spread with rillettes and top with beet relish and black pepper. Cut the bread into halves and serve with greens.

· NOTE ·

The rillettes and relish have uses beyond this tartine: Spread the fish pâté on cucumber or steamed potato slices, or garnish plum tomatoes or deviled eggs. The beet relish is great with cold meats and in a potato salad.

~PITA~
à la ratatouille et aux œufs,
sauce tahini

RATATOUILLE PITA SANDWICH

WITH CHOPPED EGGS & TAHINI SAUCE

SERVES 2

THE SMALL STREETS OF THE MARAIS NEIGHBORHOOD ARE SO CHARMING it hurts, and if you lose yourself in their maze, you will likely happen upon the tiny Jewish quarter around rue des Rosiers. It is here, among the many Ashkenazi delis, that you'll find Miznon, which quickly stole the heart of Parisians. Created by celebrated Tel Aviv chef Eyal Shani, the tiny place has just a few seats and an open kitchen churning out the most flavorful pita sandwiches I've ever tried. The big and fluffy house-made pockets are stuffed to the gills with grilled lamb, herbed chicken salad, or ratatouille and chopped hard-boiled eggs dressed with tahini sauce. (Though they are plenty satisfying, keep room for the "burnt cauliflower" served whole and deliciously charred.)

I can't give you a recipe for the high-energy ambience of Miznon, the crowd spilling out onto the narrow street and the waitstaff shouting names when orders are ready, but I can help you re-create my favorite vegetarian sandwich.

FOR THE TAHINI SAUCE

2 tablespoons tahini

1 tablespoon freshly squeezed lemon juice, or more to taste

½ teaspoon fine sea salt, or more to taste

FOR THE SANDWICHES

2 large pitas (about 3 ounces/ 85 g each)

1½ cups (225 g) Oven-Roasted Ratatouille (page 224), warm

2 Steamed Hard-Boiled Eggs (page 62), peeled and roughly chopped

Fine sea salt

MAKE THE TAHINI SAUCE: In a small bowl, stir together the tahini, lemon juice, and salt. Add 1 tablespoon water, stirring until smooth. Taste and adjust the seasoning, adding lemon juice or salt if needed.

ASSEMBLE THE SANDWICHES: Warm the pitas in the toaster. Halve them to make half-moon pockets; each person gets two half-pockets. Spoon tahini sauce into each pocket, follow with ratatouille and eggs, and add a pinch of salt. Serve immediately.

GALETTE FILLINGS

The most typical galette is *la complète*, with cooked ham, grated cheese, and a fried egg. This is what I always order, sometimes with sliced tomatoes or mushrooms. *L'andouille* is filled with slices of tripe sausage, and it makes children giggle because *andouille* also means "dummy." Their appreciation of tripe sausage generally stops there.

Dream up your own fillings using different kinds of cheese, cooked vegetables, smoked fish, etc., but don't overcomplicate it. Stick to two to three ingredients in moderate quantities so the buckwheat shines through. I also love buckwheat crêpes for dessert, with Notella (page 43) or Simple Chocolate Sauce (page 247).

PARIS HAS A LARGE COMMUNITY OF BRETON 'EXPATS.' SOME ARE RECENT
arrivals; many come from families who settled in the capital at the turn of
the twentieth century, when a brand-new train line linked Brest to Paris
and the Breton youth sought opportunities in the big city. The culture is
kept alive in part through crêperies, casual and family-friendly.

Traditional buckwheat crêpes are gluten-free and made with just
buckwheat flour, salt, and water. They are cooked on a *billig*, a wide cast-
iron cooking surface that gets you thin galettes with a lace-like, crackly
edge. To make the batter easier to cook in a skillet at home, I add an egg as
a binder. After a couple of tries, you'll know the right consistency for the
batter, and how hot your pan needs to be. Old Bretonnes spit onto their
billig to assess the temperature, I'm told.

1½ cups (200 g) buckwheat flour

1 teaspoon fine sea salt

1 large egg

Salted butter, for cooking

YOUR CHOICE OF FILLINGS

Grated cheese, cooked ham,
eggs, cooked mushrooms, baby
spinach, sliced tomatoes, tomato
sauce, sliced goat cheese . . .
(see Galette Fillings, opposite)

· NOTES ·

If the batter sizzles and dances
wildly around the skillet when
you pour it in, the pan is too hot.
Reduce the heat for the next crêpe.

If the crêpes are thick and take
a long time to cook, thin the batter
with a little water and try again.

You can cook the unfilled crêpes
beforehand, stack them on a
plate, and cover. A few moments
before serving, reheat and garnish
the crêpes.

The batter keeps for up to 3 days,
covered and refrigerated.

Prepare the batter at least 3 hours ahead, or the day before. In a bowl,
whisk together the buckwheat flour and salt. Form a well in the center
and whisk the egg in with part of the flour.

Measure 2½ cups (600 ml) cold water in a measuring cup. Pour it in
gradually, whisking until the batter is smooth. It will be fairly thin. Cover
and refrigerate for at least 3 hours or overnight. Whisk again before using.

Heat a large skillet over medium heat. Melt ½ teaspoon butter in it and
spread across the bottom with a wadded-up paper towel to absorb the
excess fat (watch your fingers). Keep the paper towel by the stove.

Ladle about ⅓ cup (80 ml) batter into the skillet and immediately swirl
the pan around to form a round and distribute the batter in a thin, even
layer. Cook over medium heat until the edges of the crêpe are set, 2 to
3 minutes. Try gently slipping a spatula underneath. If you can do it
easily, loosen the crêpe from the pan, but don't flip it. If the crêpe is still
sticking to the pan, do not force it; give it another 1 or 2 minutes and
try again.

When you are able to loosen the crêpe, add your toppings on one half
of the crêpe and cook for a few more minutes, until the crêpe is golden
underneath and the toppings are cooked as needed. Fold the free side
of the crêpe over the filling, press gently, and slide onto a plate. You can
serve these from the skillet as you make them, or keep them warm in a
140°F (60°C) oven.

~CRÊPES~
de pois chiche
à la carotte

CARROT CHICKPEA CRÊPES

MAKES 8 CRÊPES

IF YOU'RE IN PARIS DURING GANESH CHATURTHI, THE TEN-DAY HINDU festival that celebrates the elephant-headed god (the date shifts according to the Hindu lunisolar calendar), you must go to La Chapelle, the "Little India" of Paris, and take in the parade. Any time of year, the neighborhood transports visitors six thousand miles away to Sri Lanka, where most of the local Tamil community hails from. I go to fill my shopping bag with exotic roots and greens, spices and aromatic rice in bulk, and mangoes so fragrant they keep me awake at night.

Before I head home, I grab lunch and often opt for crêpes or fritters—such as these *pudlas* I've learned to cook at home. The batter is made with chickpea flour—found at Indian markets, natural foods stores, and well-stocked supermarkets—which is gluten-free. I fold in vegetables and herbs, cook them in the skillet like pancakes, and serve with yogurt and chutney.

· NOTE ·
Serve these from the skillet as you make them, or keep warm in a 170°F (75°C) oven. I like them at room temperature, too.

1¼ cups (150 g) chickpea flour

1 teaspoon fine sea salt

1 teaspoon ground cumin

1 teaspoon ground turmeric

½ teaspoon amchoor (green mango powder; optional)

1 tablespoon freshly squeezed lemon juice

1 medium carrot, finely grated

2 scallions (white and green parts), finely sliced

1 small green chile, finely chopped (seeded for less heat)

½ cup roughly chopped fresh cilantro leaves

Oil for cooking or coconut oil

Greek yogurt, for serving

Store-bought chutney, for serving (optional)

Prepare the batter at least 30 minutes and up to a day in advance. In a medium bowl, combine the chickpea flour, salt, cumin, turmeric, and amchoor (if using). Whisk in 1 cup (240 ml) water to get a smooth, lump-free batter. Cover and let rest for 30 minutes to 1 hour on the counter, or overnight in the refrigerator. The batter will thicken.

Stir in the lemon juice, carrot, scallions, chile, and cilantro.

Set a heavy-bottomed skillet over medium heat. Wait until it is hot enough to make a drop of water sizzle. Add ½ teaspoon oil and spread across the bottom of the skillet with a wadded-up paper towel to absorb the excess fat (watch your fingers). Keep the paper towel by the stove.

Ladle about ⅓ cup (80 ml) batter into the pan and spread into a 5-inch (12 cm) round using the back of the ladle. Cook until the top is just set and you are able to slip a spatula underneath with no resistance, about 1 minute. The underside should be golden brown. Flip and cook until golden on the second side, about 30 seconds. Repeat to make additional crêpes, greasing the skillet again before each one.

Serve with yogurt and chutney (if desired) for dipping.

QUICHE LORRAINE IS THE MOST CLASSIC OF FRENCH QUICHES, AND IT IS ubiquitous in Parisian bakeries and charcuteries. The flaky crust holds a silken custard, rich with the flavor of good eggs and nutmeg, and the savory, chewy jolts of diced ham and bacon bits—or, really, *lardons*, short thin strips of pork belly that are a basic punctuation of cooking in the northern half of France. In Paris, you purchase them by the weight at the butcher shop and they'll chop them in front of you as they chat about the neighbor's cat that ran away. If your local butcher won't make them, get thick-cut bacon and slice it crosswise into short matchsticks.

Quiche lorraine makes your house smell divine, or at least like my mother's kitchen, which is the same thing to me. Invite friends over for lunch on a Sunday and offer this, with a great big bowl of sharply dressed greens, and they may ask to move in with you.

~QUICHE~
lorraine

CLASSIC HAM & BACON
QUICHE

MAKES ONE 10-INCH (25 CM)
QUICHE; SERVES 4 TO 6

Tart Pastry (recipe follows)

5 slices (5 ounces/150 g) thick-cut bacon, plain or smoked, cut crosswise into short strips

4 large eggs

¾ cup (180 ml) crème fraîche or full-fat sour cream

1½ cups (360 ml) whole milk

⅛ teaspoon freshly ground black pepper

⅛ teaspoon freshly ground nutmeg

2 ounces (55 g) thick-cut ham, diced

Mixed greens, lightly dressed with Bistro Vinaigrette (page 54), for serving

Make the tart pastry and use it to line a 10-inch (25 cm) pie or quiche pan.

Preheat the oven to 400°F (200°C).

Top the dough in the pan with a sheet of parchment paper, add pie weights (or dried beans), and bake for 15 minutes.

Meanwhile, in a small dry skillet, fry the bacon strips until just browned, about 10 minutes. Drain. (Keep the rendered fat for another use.)

In a medium bowl, beat the eggs lightly with a fork. Gently stir in the crème fraîche, milk, pepper, and nutmeg; avoid beating too much air into the mixture, or the filling will puff up and then crack once baked.

Remove the tart shell from the oven and reduce the oven temperature to 300°F (150°C). Lift the parchment paper carefully and remove the pie weights.

Scatter the bacon and ham evenly over the tart shell, then slowly pour in the egg mixture without disturbing the bacon and ham. Bake until the filling is golden brown but still a little jiggly in the center, 50 to 60 minutes. Let set for at least 15 minutes before serving. Enjoy warm or at room temperature, with a salad.

TART PASTRY

Pâte brisée

**MAKES ENOUGH
TO LINE ONE
10- TO 12-INCH
(25 TO 30 CM)
TART OR
QUICHE PAN**

LET ME DISPEL A MYTH: French cooks use store-bought crusts, as evidenced by the many options offered in even the smallest Paris supermarkets. However, let me make a case for homemade pâte brisée, the little black dress of pastry, which truly comes together in minutes and elevates baked goods in a way you would not think possible.

7 ounces (200 g) all-purpose flour (about 1½ cups), plus more for rolling

½ teaspoon fine sea salt

7 tablespoons (100 g) cold unsalted butter, diced

1 large egg

Ice-cold water, if needed

· **NOTE** ·

For sweet uses, you can either roll out the dough in sugar, or sprinkle your buttered pan with sugar. In both cases, the crust will be sugar-studded and irresistibly caramelized, as for Caramelized Plum Tart (page 112).

WITH A FOOD PROCESSOR

In a food processor, combine the flour, salt, and butter. Process for 10 seconds, until you get a bread crumb–like consistency. Add the egg and process for a few more seconds, until the dough comes together into a ball. If the dough seems a little dry, mix in a little ice-cold water, 1 or 2 teaspoons at a time, until the dough does come together.

BY HAND

In a medium bowl, combine the flour and salt. Make a well in the center, add the diced butter and egg, and blend them into the flour using a pastry blender or two knives, until you're able to gather the dough into a ball. If the dough seems a little dry, mix in a little ice-cold water, 1 or 2 teaspoons at a time, until the dough comes together.

IN BOTH CASES

Tip the dough onto a clean work surface and knead lightly for a few seconds. Using a rolling pin and working on a lightly floured surface, roll the dough out and transfer to a greased 10- to 12-inch (25 to 30 cm) round tart or quiche pan, pressing it up the sides to adhere. Prick the bottom with a fork.

Cover loosely with a kitchen towel and let rest in the fridge for 30 minutes or up to a day before baking or blind-baking. This can be used to make Quiche Lorraine (page 85), Caramelized Plum Tart (page 112), or Parisian Flan (page 124).

CHEF DELPHINE ZAMPETTI RUNS HER POCKET-SIZE DELI IN WHAT USED to be a *boucherie chevaline*, a horse butcher. Horse meat was once widely consumed in Paris—it was an affordable alternative to beef—but now not so much. A few of their historic storefronts, however, have been preserved, as here: playing on the word *chevaline* and flipping a letter on the outside sign, the chef has named her operation "Chez Aline," in reference to a hit French song from the sixties. She has also kept the old-school vibe of the place, from the rack of metal hooks to the floor tiles.

In this tiny shop she crafts explosively tasty salads, sandwiches, and prepared dishes that you can eat at the counter, sitting on vintage bar stools, or take out. One of my favorites is *bonite à l'escabèche*, a dish of skipjack tuna cooked in a vibrant marinade. It is a perfect make-ahead dish that comes into its own after a night's rest in the fridge. Prepare it with any kind of sustainably fished tuna, or with sardine or mackerel fillets. I like to serve it over steamed potatoes or cauliflower, the marinade serving to season the vegetables, or in a baguette sandwich.

1 pound (450 g) ahi, yellowtail, or skipjack tuna steak from a sustainable source, cut into 1-inch (2.5 cm) cubes

1 medium yellow or red onion, finely sliced

2 medium carrots, peeled and finely sliced

3 stalks celery, finely sliced

2 garlic cloves, finely sliced

1 teaspoon fine sea salt

1 cup (240 ml) olive oil

1 teaspoon paprika

½ teaspoon chipotle powder

1 teaspoon dried thyme

Pinch of saffron (optional)

3 tablespoons sherry vinegar

Prepare the escabeche the day before serving. Preheat the oven to 400°F (200°C).

Put the fish in a medium glass or ceramic baking dish, such as an 8-inch (20 cm) square dish.

In a large skillet, combine the onion, carrots, celery, garlic, and salt and cover with the oil. Cook over medium heat, stirring regularly, until the vegetables are translucent, about 4 minutes. Add the paprika, chipotle powder, thyme, and saffron (if using). Stir and cook until softened, about 3 more minutes. Pour over the fish.

Bake until the fish is cooked through, about 15 minutes. Add the vinegar, stir, and let cool completely on the counter. Cover tightly and refrigerate overnight.

Remove from the refrigerator 30 minutes before serving.

~TAJINE~
de poisson à la chermoula

FISH TAGINE
WITH
CHERMOULA

SERVES 4 TO 6

I LIVE NOT FAR FROM THE BARBÈS OPEN-AIR MARKET, HELD ON WEDNESDAY and Saturday mornings under the elevated metro. Mostly frequented by North African immigrants, it gets insanely crowded, and I would not recommend it to the timid shopper. That said, I find it is full of charm and unbeatable for cheap produce.

I fill up on fresh, house-made harissa. The stall offers two kinds: a lemony Moroccan and a garlicky Tunisian. I like both, so I ask the attendant where he is from, and pick that one. It never fails to make him smile, and sometimes I even get a bunch of parsley or cilantro as a thank-you. With it I make chermoula: finely chopped herbs, garlic, and spices, bound together with olive oil and lemon juice. It is typically used as a condiment at the table, or to marinate fish. Cooked into this stew-like fish tagine with chickpeas, it makes for a delicious dish to serve over couscous or with flatbread.

· NOTES ·

Chermoula can also be made with all cilantro or all parsley.

You can use frozen and thawed fish.

I don't pluck the leaves from the parsley or the cilantro; I just chop the whole bunch finely, stems and all.

FOR THE CHERMOULA

½ medium lemon

1 medium bunch of fresh cilantro (about 1 ounce/30 g), a few sprigs reserved for garnish, the rest finely chopped

1 medium bunch of fresh flat-leaf parsley (about 1 ounce/30 g), finely chopped

3 garlic cloves, finely chopped

1 teaspoon ground cumin

1 teaspoon paprika

1 teaspoon ground coriander

½ teaspoon crushed red pepper flakes, or more to taste

½ teaspoon fine sea salt

1 tablespoon olive oil

FOR THE FISH

1½ pounds (700 g) white fish fillets from a sustainable source, cut into 1-inch (3 cm) pieces

2 teaspoons olive oil

2 (15-ounce/400 g) cans or jars chickpeas, rinsed and drained

FOR SERVING

Harissa

Flatbread wedges or couscous (page 198)

1 lemon, cut into 6 wedges

MAKE THE CHERMOULA AT LEAST 1 HOUR AND UP TO A DAY BEFORE COOKING: Grate the zest of the lemon into a mortar or sturdy bowl, and squeeze in the juice of the half lemon; you should get about 2 tablespoons (30 ml) juice. Add the chopped cilantro, parsley, garlic, cumin, paprika, coriander, pepper flakes, salt, and olive oil. Pound with a pestle, or use the bottom of a clean spice jar.

MARINATE THE FISH: Put the fish in a nonreactive container with a lid. Add the chermoula and stir well to coat. Cover and refrigerate for at least 45 minutes, or overnight.

In a heavy-bottomed pot, heat the 2 teaspoons olive oil over medium heat. Add the fish with whatever chermoula clings to it, reserving what remains in the container. Cover and cook for 3 to 4 minutes. Add the chickpeas and remaining chermoula, and cook uncovered until the fish is just done, 2 to 3 minutes more.

TO SERVE, garnish with the reserved cilantro. Set out harissa and lemon wedges for guests to adjust the seasoning. Offer a side of flatbread or couscous.

ROAST CHICKEN
WITH HERBED BUTTER & CROUTONS

SERVES 4

TO THE FRENCH, NOTHING SAYS "SUNDAY LUNCH" LIKE ROAST CHICKEN, and in Paris, there are many ways to make it happen. You can go out to a restaurant like Drouant where they serve it as a Sunday exclusive with a tray of thick fries and a large bowl of lettuce. You can get it from a market-street *rôtisserie*, where they tend to dozens of birds on rotating spits, basting them all morning so they are fall-off-the-bone tender and dark amber when the church bells strike eleven.

But roasting a chicken at home is a rewarding enterprise with a few simple tricks—rubbing the inside of the skin with butter and herbs, and stuffing the bird with croutons. In fact, the bird tastes even better if you prep it the night before and roast it in midmorning. This gives you time to trim and steam French green beans—the slimmer kind—to serve with a drizzle of the cooking juices, as my mother did every Sunday during *haricot vert* season.

4 tablespoons (55 g) unsalted butter, slightly softened

½ cup (20 g) chopped fresh herbs, such as flat-leaf parsley, chives, chervil, basil, or cilantro

1 teaspoon fine sea salt

½ teaspoon dried garlic flakes

1 whole chicken (about 3½ pounds/1.6 kg)

1⅔ cups (85 g) cubed day-old bread

· **NOTE** ·
The chicken can be buttered and stuffed up to a day in advance. Wrap tightly in plastic wrap and refrigerate.

Preheat the oven to 450°F (230°C).

In a medium bowl, mash together the butter, herbs, salt, and garlic flakes.

Put the chicken breast side up, neck end facing you, on a clean work surface. Slip a clean hand under the skin, starting at the base of the neck, and work your hand further in gently, lifting the skin over each breast and down over each thigh, without tearing. Once the skin is loosened, slip in two-thirds of the herbed butter (reserve the rest for the croutons), pushing it under the skin to coat the breasts and thighs evenly.

Add the bread cubes to the remaining herbed butter and stir to coat. Stuff the buttered cubes inside the cavity, and tie the chicken with kitchen string around the drumstick ends and wings to hold its shape.

Put the chicken breast side up in a baking dish. Roast for 20 minutes.

Loosen the chicken gently from the bottom of the dish. Flip to expose the back and baste with the juices. Roast for 20 minutes more.

Loosen and flip the chicken so the breast faces up again, baste with the juices, and roast until the skin is golden brown and crackly, a final 20 minutes. A meat thermometer inserted into the thickest part of the thigh should register 165°F (75°C). Remove from the oven, cover with foil, and let rest for 10 to 15 minutes.

Carve the chicken and serve with the croutons and cooking juices.

CHICKEN COLOMBO

WITH PLANTAINS

SERVES 4

IN ADDITION TO LA MÉTROPOLE, OR MAINLAND FRANCE, THE COUNTRY comprises overseas territories such as the Caribbean islands of Martinique and Guadeloupe, which became French colonies in the seventeenth century, and were soon populated with African slaves. While this painful history lies under the surface, there are many back-and-forth exchanges, both cultural and economic, that remain a silver lining.

Paris is home to a large Creole community with a rich culinary heritage that has been shaped by the many populations who traveled through the French Caribbean over the centuries. The East Indian influence is evident in the use of spices, and the signature dish, the colombo, is a meat stew flavored with *poudre de colombo*, a curry powder named after the capital of Sri Lanka. You'll find it at Caribbean markets or online; you can also mix your own or use your favorite curry powder.

There are many colombo variations, but just two secrets to success: the first is to marinate the meat overnight; the other is to include *graines à roussir*, a mix of seeds you'll infuse in the cooking oil. The following recipe is quick to assemble and well balanced, and as it simmers on your stove it will fill your kitchen with the scents of a Creole kitchen.

· VARIATIONS ·

The potato and onion are a mainstay, but you can mix and match other vegetables depending on what's in season: Eggplant, bell peppers, sweet potatoes, pumpkin, chayote squash, carrots, and okra are all in keeping with the French Caribbean background of this dish.

DIY COLOMBO POWDER

Combine 2 tablespoons each cumin seeds and coriander seeds; 2 teaspoons each brown mustard seeds, fenugreek seeds, black peppercorns, dried garlic flakes, and uncooked rice; and 3 whole cloves. Toast in a dry skillet over medium heat until fragrant, about 2 minutes. Remove from the heat, let cool completely, then grind finely in a clean spice grinder. Stir in 2 tablespoons ground turmeric and 1 tablespoon ground ginger. Keep in a jar with an airtight lid. Use as you would any curry powder: with vegetables, meat and poultry, or fish.

2⅔ pounds (1.2 kg) skin-on bone-in chicken thighs and drumsticks

¼ cup (60 ml) freshly squeezed lime juice (about 2 limes)

3 tablespoons colombo powder (see DIY Colombo Powder, left) or curry powder

2 tablespoons neutral oil, such as sunflower seed, grapeseed, or canola

Fine sea salt

½ teaspoon fenugreek seeds

½ teaspoon cumin seeds

½ teaspoon yellow mustard seeds

½ teaspoon fennel seeds

2 medium plantains (not too ripe), peeled and cut into slices ½ inch (1.25 cm) thick

1 medium potato, peeled and cut into 1-inch (2.5 cm) cubes

1 medium zucchini, cut into 1-inch (2.5 cm) pieces

1 medium yellow onion, finely sliced

1 to 2 small fresh red chiles (optional), finely chopped (seeded for less heat)

1 bay leaf

Steamed long-grain rice, for serving

Chopped fresh flat-leaf parsley, for serving

Lime wedges, for serving

Start 4 hours ahead or preferably the day before serving. Put the chicken in a large nonreactive bowl. Add the lime juice, 1 tablespoon of the colombo spice mix, 1 tablespoon of the oil, and 1 teaspoon fine sea salt. Turn the chicken to coat well. Cover and refrigerate for at least 3 hours, or overnight.

In a large heavy-bottomed pot, heat the remaining 1 tablespoon oil over medium heat. Add the graines à roussir: fenugreek, cumin, mustard, and fennel seeds. Cover, wait to hear the seeds pop, and cook for 30 seconds. Remove from the heat, scoop out most of the seeds (it's okay if a few remain behind), and set aside in a small bowl to cool.

Return the pot to medium heat. Lift the chicken from the container (reserve the marinade) and put the pieces skin side down in a single layer. Cook until golden on both sides, flipping halfway through, about 10 minutes.

Add the plantains, potato, zucchini, onion, chiles, if using, and ½ teaspoon salt. Return the seeds to the pot. Stir in the remaining 2 tablespoons colombo powder and the bay leaf. Add the reserved marinade and enough water to barely cover the meat and vegetables, about 4 cups (1 liter). Cover, bring to a simmer, and cook until the chicken is very tender, about 40 minutes.

Taste and adjust the seasoning. Discard the bay leaf. Serve over steamed rice, with a sprinkle of chopped parsley and lime wedges for squeezing.

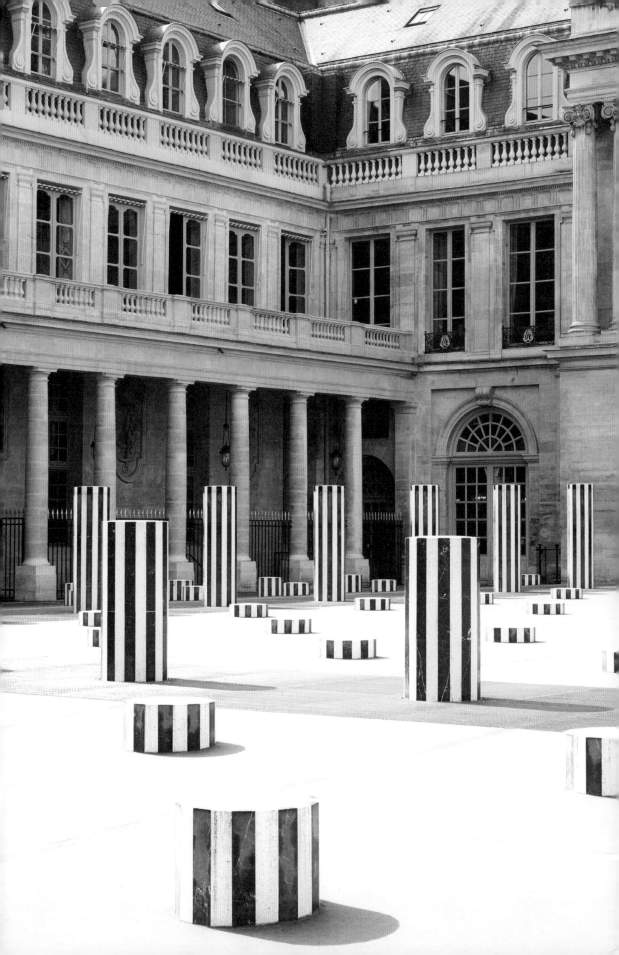

STEAK
WITH
PEPPERCORN
SAUCE

SERVES 4 TO 6

MOST FRENCH RESTAURANTS IN PARIS OFFER AN ITEM THAT FALLS INTO the *steak-frites* category, either literally (grilled piece of beef, French fries, check!) or as a riff (the beef isn't grilled but cooked sous-vide, the potatoes aren't fries but *pommes soufflées* . . .). I like the literal version best of all, and order it from classic bistros and brasseries, where they give a choice of sauce, such as *sauce au poivre*, *béarnaise*, or *sauce au bleu*.

1½ pounds (680 g) boneless beef steak (1 to 1½ inches/2.5 to 4 cm thick), your choice of cut (see Steak Cuts, left)

Fine sea salt

2 teaspoons neutral oil, such as sunflower seed, grapeseed, or canola

⅓ cup (80 ml) Cognac or other brandy

5 tablespoons (80 g) unsalted butter, diced

⅓ cup (80 g) heavy cream

1 tablespoon white or black peppercorns, cracked (see How to Crack Peppercorns, left)

Amazing Oven Fries (opposite), for serving

HOW TO CRACK PEPPERCORNS

The mix of bigger and smaller pieces in cracked peppercorns creates texture and flavor in the sauce. Crack peppercorns in a mortar with a pestle; or use a grinder that gives you the option of a large grind; or put them in a pile on a cutting board, top with a heavy pot, and apply your weight to crush.

STEAK CUTS

It is tricky to recommend a cut of beef for authentic steak-frites. First, it is a matter of taste to favor short-fiber or long-fiber cuts, heavily marbled or leaner meat, tenderness over bold flavor. Second, French butchers have their own meat-cutting diagrams and there is no equivalent to many of their imaginatively named cuts, such as *poire* (pear), *merlan* (whiting), or *araignée* (spider).

I like flank steak, rib eye, strip, and hanger (*onglet* in French—my favorite). Better to pick thicker steaks that you'll slice into servings rather than thin individual steaks that will be overdone before the outside gets crusty.

About an hour before serving, remove the meat from the refrigerator and pat dry with paper towels. Sprinkle all over with 1 teaspoon salt.

In a large heavy pan, preferably cast iron, heat the oil over medium-high heat until it is just beginning to smoke. Add the meat and cook without disturbing for about 3 minutes until a golden crust forms. Flip and repeat on the other side. Flip again and then cook, flipping and basting with the juices every 20 to 30 seconds, until the meat is browned on the outside and cooked to your liking, a few minutes more. If you have a meat thermometer, aim for 130°F (55°C) for medium rare.

Transfer the steak to a cutting board, preferably with grooves around the edges to collect the juices. Cover with foil and let rest while you prepare the sauce.

Reduce the heat under the pan to medium. Pour in the Cognac, add ½ teaspoon salt, and scrape the bottom of the pan with a spatula to loosen the good bits. Stir in the butter to emulsify, and cook for 1 minute. Add the cream and cracked peppercorns and stir until warmed through.

Cut the meat into servings if needed and divide among 4 to 6 plates. Spoon some of the sauce over the meat. Serve with the fries and the remaining sauce in a warmed bowl or small pitcher.

FRENCH FRIES ARE A POPULAR SIDE IN PARIS RESTAURANTS. THEY MAY BE thick or thin, light blond or browning at the edges; what's important is that they be *faites maison* (homemade, not frozen), crisp on the outside and tender in the middle, and full of a sweet yet nutty potato flavor. Because I have an open kitchen, frying—which ends up imbuing the whole apartment with its scent—is not my method of choice. I have found a way to make golden and crunchy French fries in the oven: First I blanch the potatoes briefly and then drain them before returning them to the saucepan and shaking them for a few seconds. Making their surface a little fuzzy fosters the formation of a magnificent crust in the oven.

2¼ pounds (1 kg) white potatoes (any kind), peeled or simply scrubbed

Fine sea salt

2 tablespoons vegetable oil or rendered duck fat

Preheat the oven to 425°F (220°C).

Cut the potatoes into long strips, each about ½ inch (1.25 cm) thick. Put in a large saucepan, cover with cold water, and add 1 teaspoon salt. Cover and bring to a simmer over high heat. Reduce the heat to medium and simmer for 5 minutes.

Meanwhile, drizzle the oil or fat onto a rimmed baking sheet and put in the oven to heat.

Drain the potatoes, return to the saucepan, and put the lid on the saucepan. Holding up the saucepan and lid firmly with oven-mitt-covered hands, shake for 5 seconds, until the surface of the potatoes is fuzzy.

Remove the baking sheet from the oven, carefully pour the potatoes onto the sheet (the hot fat may splatter), sprinkle with 1 teaspoon salt, and toss to coat with the oil. Bake for 20 minutes, flip the fries over, and bake, until golden and crusty, another 10 to 20 minutes.

Serve immediately.

· **VARIATIONS** ·

Cut the potatoes into cubes rather than fries.

Add 1 teaspoon finely chopped rosemary, fresh or dried, just before shaking.

AS AN EVEN EASIER ALTERNATIVE TO STEAK WITH PEPPERCORN SAUCE (page 96), this grilled steak is adorned with *beurre maître d'hôtel*, which belongs to the family of compound butters, made by mixing flavorings into butter. The possibilities are endless, both in the ingredients added and in the ways to serve the resulting *beurre composé*: cold with crunchy crudités such as radishes, lightly spread on crostini or in sandwiches, or softly melting on a piece of steamed fish. It's hard to imagine how something so simple can bring such an air of sophistication, but there it is. Keep a log of this parsley/shallot butter in your freezer or fridge, and adopt the smug air of the cook who can whip up a bistro classic in minutes.

~STEAK~
au beurre maître d'hôtel

STEAK
WITH
MAÎTRE D'HÔTEL
BUTTER

SERVES 4 TO 6

8 tablespoons (115 g) high-quality unsalted butter, slightly softened

3 tablespoons (20 g) finely chopped shallot

3 tablespoons (10 g) finely chopped fresh flat-leaf parsley

1 teaspoon freshly squeezed lemon juice

Fine sea salt

1½ pounds (680 g) boneless beef steak, your choice of cut (see Steak Cuts, page 96), 1 to 1½ inches (2.5 to 4 cm) thick

2 teaspoons neutral oil, such as sunflower seed, grapeseed, or canola

Amazing Oven Fries (page 97)

Make the compound butter the day before serving. In a medium bowl, combine the butter, shallot, parsley, lemon juice, and ½ teaspoon salt. Using a wooden spoon, mash the flavorings into the butter. Scrape onto a sheet of parchment paper or plastic wrap and roll into a log about 1½ inches (4 cm) in diameter and 5 inches (13 cm) long. Wrap tightly and refrigerate until ready to serve.

About 1 hour before serving, remove the meat from the refrigerator and pat dry with paper towels. Sprinkle all over with 1 teaspoon salt.

In a large heavy pan, preferably cast iron, heat the oil over medium-high heat until it is just beginning to smoke. Add the meat and cook without disturbing for about 3 minutes, until a golden crust forms. Flip and repeat on the other side. Flip again and then cook, flipping and basting with the juices every 20 to 30 seconds, until the meat is browned on the outside and cooked to your liking, a few minutes more. If you have a meat thermometer, aim for 130°F (55°C) for medium rare.

Transfer the steak to a cutting board, preferably one with grooves to collect the juices. Cover with foil and let rest.

Unwrap the butter and cut 4 to 6 rounds (depending on the number of servings), each about ⅓ inch (1 cm) thick. (You will have more than you need here; reserve extra for other uses.)

Slice the meat into servings as needed, transfer to warmed plates, and put a round of butter to melt on each serving. Serve with fries.

CHOCOLATE
MOUSSE

IN PARIS, YOU WILL SPOT CHOCOLATE MOUSSE IN OLD-SCHOOL STEMMED cups in the dessert fridges of brasseries, and in small tubs at pâtisseries. I like it best of all when I'm invited to lunch at the home of friends or relatives and, as I help clear the plates, it becomes apparent that someone has been beating a lot of egg whites and chopping a lot of chocolate to fill a big salad bowl with mousse, fluffy and perfectly set. Oh, the anticipation that builds as the host or hostess dips a big spoon in and carves out dollops to distribute among guests!

Here's my recipe for classic chocolate mousse. You can serve it on its own, or with seasonal fresh fruit (especially berries or pears) or butter cookies for scooping.

· **NOTE** ·

Chocolate mousse is made with raw eggs, so make sure you use extra-fresh ones. Do not serve it to very young children, pregnant women, or anyone with a compromised immune system.

7 ounces (200 g) high-quality bittersweet chocolate (60 to 70% cacao), couverture if available, finely chopped

¾ cup (180 ml) heavy cream

4 large eggs, separated (see Note)

¼ teaspoon fine sea salt

⅛ teaspoon cream of tartar

3 tablespoons (35 g) sugar

Start 3 hours or up to a day before serving. Have ready six ½-cup (120 ml) ramekins or glass tumblers, or a 3-cup (720 ml) serving bowl.

Put the chocolate in a large heatproof bowl. In a small saucepan, bring the cream to a boil. Pour over the chocolate and stir with a spatula until smooth and shiny.

In the bowl of a stand mixer fitted with the whisk attachment (or in a large bowl if using a hand mixer or whisk), combine the egg whites with the salt and cream of tartar. Whip on medium-high speed until the whites form medium-soft peaks, about 1 minute. Continue beating and add the sugar in four additions, counting 15 seconds between each. Whip to stiff peaks. The meringue should be glossy and white.

Whisk the egg yolks into the chocolate mixture one by one, until fully incorporated. Whisk in one-third of the egg whites to loosen the texture. Using a spatula, fold in the remaining egg whites in two additions, working in a circular, vertical motion to avoid deflating the egg whites.

Divide among the prepared ramekins, cover with plastic wrap, and refrigerate for at least 2 hours or overnight. Serve cold.

~MILLE-FEUILLE~
framboise et citron

RASPBERRY LEMON MILLE-FEUILLE

SERVES 4

MILLE-FEUILLE ("ONE THOUSAND LAYERS") IS A CLASSIC FRENCH PASTRY constructed from sheets of puff pastry sandwiched together with pastry cream, and sometimes with berries. It is one of the most satisfying—and messiest—of treats, as the fork crashes through the construction and smooshes the cream out the sides. My favorite place to order one is chocolatier Jacques Genin's tea salon in the hip Upper Marais, where you can plop yourself into a cushy armchair while the pastry elves upstairs construct the perfect mille-feuille just for you; the best ones are freshly assembled, for an optimal contrast between the crisp pastry and the smooth cream.

I love to surprise weekend lunch guests with this refreshing version, filled with lemon curd and raspberries. I prepare the curd and puff pastry the day before, then bake and slice the pastry in the morning. The assembly is done at the last minute, right before my friends' hungry eyes.

· NOTES ·
You will have a bit more lemon curd than you need: Keep in the fridge for spreading on toast or scones. Use within 3 to 4 days.

If you prefer not to make your own lemon curd, use ⅔ cup (160 ml) store-bought lemon curd.

· VARIATION ·
Fill your mille-feuilles with Chantilly Whipped Cream (page 143) and quartered strawberries.

2½ lemons

½ cup (100 g) granulated sugar

1 tablespoon cornstarch

2 large eggs

Easy Puff Pastry (recipe follows), or 12 ounces (340 g) store-bought all-butter puff pastry

7 ounces (200 g) raspberries, thawed if frozen

Powdered sugar

Prepare the lemon curd at least 2 hours and up to 1 day before serving. Grate the zest from 1 lemon into a medium nonreactive saucepan. Juice all of the lemons and measure out ⅓ cup plus 1 tablespoon (95 ml) juice. Add it to the pan, along with the granulated sugar. Whisk the cornstarch with 1 tablespoon water until smooth and then stir into the pan. Set over low heat, stirring regularly with a heatproof spatula, just until the sugar dissolves. Set aside to cool for 5 minutes.

In a medium nonreactive bowl, beat the eggs. Whisk in the warm lemon mixture, adding it little by little to avoid scrambling the eggs. Pour everything back into the saucepan and cook over medium-low heat, stirring constantly with a spatula and scraping the bottom and sides of the pan well, until the curd thickens. It is ready when the spatula leaves a clear trace at the bottom of the pan, about 5 minutes.

Strain through a fine-mesh sieve into a heatproof container. Cool completely, then cover and refrigerate until chilled. It will set as it cools.

Roll out the puff pastry between two sheets of parchment paper to form a rectangle about 8 × 9½ inches (20 × 24 cm). Refrigerate until ready to bake.

(recipe continues)

Preheat the oven to 400°F (200°C).

Put the puff pastry with its sheets of parchment paper on a baking sheet and top with another baking sheet to weigh it down. Bake for 25 minutes. Remove the top baking sheet and top parchment paper and bake until golden brown, about 5 minutes more.

Slide the parchment paper and pastry onto a cutting board and let cool for 15 minutes. Using a serrated knife, cut into a neat 8 × 9-inch (20 × 23 cm) rectangle. Cut in half to get two tall and narrow rectangles, then cut each of these into 6 small rectangles 4 × 1½ inches (10 × 4 cm). You will get 12 rectangles total.

To assemble, put one rectangle of puff pastry on a plate. Spread with 1 tablespoon lemon curd, top with a layer of raspberries, then dot the berries with 1 teaspoon lemon curd. Put a second rectangle of puff pastry on top, pressing gently to adhere. Repeat with another layer of lemon curd and raspberries, and top with a third and final rectangle of puff pastry. Assemble 3 more mille-feuilles.

Balance chopsticks or bamboo skewers at an angle on top of the mille-feuilles, to serve as stencils for diagonal stripes. Dust with powdered sugar, then remove the chopsticks carefully.

Serve immediately, or reserve in the refrigerator for up to 1 hour, tops. Remove from the fridge 30 minutes before serving.

EASY PUFF PASTRY

Pâte feuilletée facile

MAKES
11 OUNCES
(325 G)

THIS IS A LIFE-CHANGER OF A RECIPE, a fuss-free formula for puff pastry that I learned from my friend Lucy Vanel, who runs the Plum cooking school in Lyon. It does not involve rolling out the butter and enclosing it in a layer of dough, nor does it confine you to the kitchen with incessant refrigeration steps. Instead, you cut the butter into the flour to form a rough dough, then do four rounds of rolling, folding, and turning, but without refrigerating the dough each time. *Voilà*: homemade puff pastry in about 15 minutes, without sacrificing flavor.

· NOTES ·

Puff pastry is only as good as the butter you use; this is a good time to splurge on European-style butter with big flavor and high butterfat content.

This is best prepared in a cool kitchen, on a cool work surface, using light and assertive gestures to prevent overheating the dough. Don't attempt it when the oven is on.

If you find the dough becomes sticky at any point, refrigerate for 30 minutes to cool again.

4½ ounces (125 g) all-purpose flour (about 1 cup), chilled if you've had the foresight, plus more for rolling

10 tablespoons (140 g) high-quality unsalted butter (see Notes), chilled and diced

¼ teaspoon fine sea salt

¼ cup (60 ml) ice-cold water or milk

In a medium bowl, combine the flour, butter, and salt. Using a pastry blender or two knives, cut the butter into the flour, stopping when the mixture looks crumbly but fairly even, with the average piece of butter about the size of a large pea. (Don't overblend, or you won't get the puffy effect.)

Turn out onto a clean and cool work surface and form a well in the center. Pour in the water and work it into the flour and butter mixture—I use a bench scraper but a wooden spoon will do. Knead lightly, just enough so that the dough comes together into a ball, and shape into a rough square. There should be little pieces of butter visible in the dough.

Flour your work surface lightly. Using a lightly floured rolling pin, roll out the dough into a rectangle about 10 inches (25 cm) long. Add more flour as needed to prevent sticking. Brush to remove excess flour and fold the dough in three, like a letter, so the top and bottom overlap, dusting again after the first fold. Give the dough a quarter of a turn, and repeat the rolling and folding steps. Repeat until you've rolled and folded a total of four times. You should get a neat rectangular or square pad of dough.

Put the dough on a plate, cover, and refrigerate for at least 1 hour or overnight before using. If the dough seems too stiff when you take it out of the fridge, let it come to room temperature for 15 to 20 minutes before using.

MARKET STREETS FORM THE BACKBONE OF PARIS NEIGHBORHOODS, and when locals need an escape from their small apartments, this is where they gravitate. They'll say, "Oh, let's go get some bread," then bump into a neighbor, sit down at a café for a bit, get hungry, see it's almost time for dinner, and run a week's worth of errands, hopping from shop to shop, before heading home.

They will hit the produce stall, its goods spilling out artfully on the sidewalk display and tantalizing passersby with just-ripe fruit. It is hard to keep walking when the strawberries are out . . . or the cantaloupes or peaches. What gets me every time is the smell of oranges cutting through the winter air, promising fresh squeezed juice and a divine Moroccan-style salad.

This recipe is based on one my produce vendor shared while wrapping up my oranges. "Cut thin slices," he instructed. "And sprinkle them with a little bit of sugar. Not too much! My oranges are very sweet! Also some orange blossom water. You have it? Good. And some mint."

This deceptively simple salad is even better if it has a chance to sit for a little while.

4 large juicy oranges (or grapefruits or tangerines)

2 teaspoons sugar or honey

½ teaspoon ground cinnamon

2 to 3 teaspoons orange blossom water, to taste

6 fresh mint leaves

3 tablespoons raw pistachios, roughly chopped

Use a sharp knife to slice off the very top and very bottom of each orange, just enough to expose the flesh. Now, with the fruit resting on its stable base on the cutting board, slice off a strip of peel from top edge to bottom edge, running the blade along the curve of the orange to remove the peel and pith and cutting away as little of the juicy flesh as possible. Work your way around strip by strip, until you've sliced off all the peel and pith. Trim any small bits of pith you missed and pour the juices that collect on the cutting board into a small saucepan. Squeeze the pieces of peel into the pan; you won't get very much, but I hate to waste anything.

Cut the oranges horizontally to form thin, flower-shaped slices, each about ¼ inch (6 mm) thick. Arrange in an overlapping pattern on a serving platter.

Add the sugar and cinnamon to the pan. Bring to a simmer, stirring to dissolve the sugar. Stir in the orange blossom water, then pour over the oranges. Cover and refrigerate for at least 1 hour, and up to 4.

Stack the slices of mint together, roll tightly, and thinly slice crosswise. Scatter the mint and pistachios over the oranges and serve.

~ÎLES FLOTTANTES~
aux fraises et au caramel

FLOATING ISLANDS

WITH CARAMEL & STRAWBERRIES

SERVES 6

IN PARIS BRASSERIES AT LUNCHTIME, MOST CUSTOMERS NEED TO GET back to work and expect brisk service. If they still want to end their meal on a sweet note, they will take a quick look at the refrigerated dessert case in the corner and point to the treat of their choice, asking for it alongside *un café et l'addition!* (An espresso and the check!) Among the classic French desserts typically featured you will find: some sort of seasonal fruit salad, Chocolate Mousse (page 100), crème caramel, and my childhood favorite, the floating island. The "island" is a cloud-like dollop of beaten egg whites floating in a pool of vanilla crème anglaise, drizzled with liquid caramel. As the spoon digs into the foamy island and plunges into the custard, it comes back with the perfect creamy bite that dissolves on the tongue. In the springtime, I add sliced strawberries for extra freshness.

FOR THE FLOATING ISLANDS

3 large egg whites

¼ teaspoon cream of tartar

¼ teaspoon fine sea salt

3 tablespoons (40 g) sugar

Vanilla Custard Sauce
(recipe follows)

FOR THE CARAMEL

¼ cup (50 g) granulated sugar

1 teaspoon freshly squeezed lemon juice

FOR SERVING

1 cup (120 g) hulled and halved strawberries

· **NOTE** ·
You can cook the egg whites in the microwave: Form 6 mounds of meringue on a plate, and microwave on high for 30 to 40 seconds.

· **VARIATION** ·
Drizzle with Simple Chocolate Sauce (page 247) instead of caramel.

MAKE THE FLOATING ISLANDS: Preheat the oven to 250°F (120°C) and have ready six ½-cup (120 ml) ramekins.

In the bowl of a stand mixer fitted with the whisk attachment (or in a large bowl if using a hand mixer or whisk), combine the egg whites, cream of tartar, and salt. Whisk the egg whites on medium speed until foamy. Whisk in 1 tablespoon of the sugar, and continue whisking on medium-high speed as you slowly sprinkle in the remaining 2 tablespoons sugar. The egg whites are ready when they are glossy and form stiff peaks.

Divide the egg whites among the ramekins and bake until set and doubled in size, 10 to 12 minutes.

Run a thin-bladed knife neatly around each meringue "island" and flip carefully onto a plate. Ladle ⅓ cup (80 ml) of the vanilla custard sauce into each of 6 dessert cups and add the meringues. You can also serve the meringues in a large serving bowl with all the vanilla custard. This can be prepared up to 3 hours in advance. Cover loosely with plastic wrap and refrigerate.

Just before serving, make the caramel: In a small, heavy-bottomed saucepan, heat the granulated sugar over medium heat. Allow the sugar to melt without stirring until it forms a light caramel. Carefully pour in the lemon juice (the hot caramel will splatter) and then stir into the caramel with a spoon. (The acid in the lemon juice will prevent the caramel from hardening as it cools.)

To serve, drizzle the caramel over the floating islands. Scatter the strawberries all around.

VANILLA CUSTARD SAUCE

Crème anglaise

MAKES
2 CUPS
(480 ML)

CRÈME ANGLAISE ("ENGLISH CREAM") is the go-to embellishment for many desserts served at Paris brasseries and tearooms: Order a slice of chocolate fondant or apple cake, and it will come in a silky pool of crème anglaise. The textbook recipe involves multiple egg yolks and can be tricky to get right. I learned from my mother, who learned from her mother, a more forgiving way to make crème anglaise using a single egg and cornstarch for thickening.

2½ cups (600 ml) whole milk

1 vanilla bean, split lengthwise, or 2 teaspoons pure vanilla extract

1 large egg

⅓ cup (65 g) sugar

3 tablespoons cornstarch

Prepare the crème anglaise at least 4 hours ahead, or the day before serving. Set a fine-mesh sieve over a bowl.

Place the milk in a medium saucepan. Scrape the vanilla seeds out of the vanilla bean and add them and the pod to the pan. Bring to a simmer over medium heat.

In a medium bowl, whisk together the egg and sugar. Whisk in the cornstarch until blended.

When the milk simmers, remove from the heat. Whisk ½ cup (120 ml) of the heated milk mixture into the egg mixture. Pour the warmed egg mixture back into the saucepan and return to medium-low heat. Cook, stirring constantly with a wooden spoon, for a few minutes. Scrape the bottom and sides of the pan well, and keep the heat low enough to prevent the milk from boiling. The custard is ready when it coats the spoon: Drag your finger through the sauce on the back of the spoon; it should leave a neat trace. It should take about 4 minutes to reach that point.

Strain the custard through the sieve into the bowl. Cover loosely with plastic wrap and let cool for 2 hours on the counter, then cover tightly and refrigerate until chilled, at least 2 hours or overnight.

~TARTE~
aux prunes caramélisée

CARAMELIZED
PLUM TART

SERVES 8

· NOTES ·

I recommend a metal tart pan with a removable bottom: Metal conducts heat best, and you can expose the sides of the tart in the final baking phase for optimal, Petits Mitrons–like caramelization. If you don't have one, the next best thing is a metal tart pan without a removable bottom.

I like to use a mix of two or three varieties of plums if available. You can use frozen plums straight from the freezer, without thawing.

YOU MAY KNOW RUE LEPIC FROM THE MOVIE *AMÉLIE*. IT IS HARD TO imagine a more charming market street, complete with a cheesemonger, a butcher shop, a fish stall, a spice vendor, a charcuterie, a *rôtisserie*, and more specialty shops than you can shake a baguette at. I showcase it on my tasting tours of Montmartre, and always pause at Les Petits Mitrons ("the baker's apprentices"). The pink-and-blue pastry shop has stopped passersby in their tracks since 1982 with its display of fruit tarts arranged on round cooling racks, seemingly straight out of a French grandmother's oven: perfectly imperfect, with jagged edges and simple patterns of seasonal fruits you would swear were picked from a garden in the back. Even more irresistible than the fruits is the sugar-studded, heavily caramelized, crunchy rim. The secret to this crust is a closely guarded one, but I created a copycat recipe.

I like to make this tart in late summer to show off the rainbow range of French plums: purple *quetsches*, green *reine-claudes*, yellow *mirabelles*. That said, it can be made with any combination of seasonal fruits: berries, figs, cherries, stone fruits, apples, pears . . .

2 teaspoons (10 g) unsalted butter

¼ cup (50 g) sugar

Tart Pastry (page 86)

1¾ pounds (800 g) just-ripe, small plums (see Notes)

¼ cup (60 ml) apricot jam

Grease a 10-inch (25 cm) metal tart pan with a removable bottom (see Notes) with the butter, and sprinkle the bottom and sides evenly with the sugar. Roll out the pâte brisée and line the pan with it, trimming the excess with a roll of the pin. Let rest for 30 minutes in the refrigerator.

Preheat the oven to 425°F (220°C). (If your oven has a mode where the heat comes primarily from the bottom heating element, use this; it will foster a deeper caramelization of the crust.)

Halve and pit the plums. If your plums are very small (1 inch/2.5 cm), just leave them as halves; otherwise cut them into quarters or sixths. Arrange the plums skin side down on the dough in a circular pattern, starting from the outside, overlapping slightly; the plums will shrink slightly as they bake. Alternate plum colors if using a mix. Bake for 20 minutes.

While the tart is baking, in a small saucepan, heat the apricot jam over low heat. Strain through a fine-mesh sieve into a bowl to remove pieces of skin.

Remove the tart from the oven (but leave the oven on). Remove the sides of the tart pan. Using a pastry brush and the strained apricot jam, glaze the sides of the tart, outside and in, and the top of the fruit. Return to the oven until darkly caramelized, 5 to 10 minutes. Transfer to a rack to cool completely.

LA MAISON QUATREHOMME

≡ Three Generations of Cheesemongers ≡

CHEESE IS ITS OWN FOOD GROUP TO THE FRENCH. SERVED BETWEEN THE main course and dessert (*not* as an appetizer), it is considered with passion and reverence.

There is no dearth of cheese shops in Paris; every greenmarket and market street offers several. But Maison Quatrehomme is a cut above the rest, both in the quality of the selection and the skill with which they age their cheeses. This is the difference between simple *fromagers*, who order ready-to-eat cheeses and sell them right away, and *fromagers-affineurs,* who buy young cheeses from cheesemakers and age them in their own cellars, watching over them tenderly, brushing or rubbing them with various concoctions, tasting them daily, and only bringing up to the shop perfectly ripe specimens.

The passion for this process runs in the Quatrehomme family. The original location on rue de Sèvres, close to the Bon Marché department store, was first opened in 1953 by Claude and Aliette. When they retired in 1978, their son, Alain, took over with his wife, Marie, who became so proficient in the work that she applied for, and won, the prestigious title of Meilleur Ouvrier de France. This is awarded to the "best craftsmen in France" after an arduous selection process. She was the first woman ever to be named in a food category.

Their own daughter and son, Nathalie and Maxime Quatrehomme, both in their early thirties, run the business now. They are infusing it with their own energy and fresh ideas, devoting their vacation time to the hunt for cheese gems and talented young producers. At the same time, they are intentional about maintaining the mom-and-pop vibe of the shop—the oldest customers have known them since they were toddling about—and their three other locations.

The head-spinning display of two hundred seasonal cheeses, most of them farm-made from raw milk, includes classics and lesser-known finds. The Quatrehomme family supplies forty of the most prestigious hotels and restaurants in the city, and even ship their goods abroad, to cheese fans in Hong Kong and Brazil.

AFTERNOON

L'APRÈS-MIDI

Un après-midi à Paris
Que je garde près de moi
—PHILIPPE KATERINE

THE REAL DIFFICULTY IN NAVIGATING THE PARIS FOOD
scene is to eat just the right-size lunch so you can start feeling hungry again in mid- to late afternoon, when *le goûter* rolls around. This mini-meal's popularity stems from a French reminiscence of afterschool snacks—which few grown-ups abandon when their school days are over. And since Parisians typically have dinner late, around 8 or 9 p.m., the need for something to tide them over until the evening meal is, you know, real.

Le goûter is a prime moment for indulgence, for sweetness and conjuring up childhood memories. It is the time to push bakery doors open and choose whatever treat calls at you from the display case; to bite into a warm apple turnover as you walk from one appointment to the next, brushing flaky crumbs from the front of your jacket; to get a cup of ice cream by the river or a crisp waffle from the carousel stand; to meet a friend and share a pastry and a cup of hot chocolate at an iconic tea salon.

~MADELEINES~
au thé Earl Grey

EARL GREY
MADELEINES

**MAKES 3 DOZEN MEDIUM
MADELEINES**

THE FRENCH HAVE A LONG HISTORY OF TEA APPRECIATION. IT WAS introduced as early as the mid-seventeenth century and was quickly adopted by the elites: Madame de Sévigné, who documented her life in vividly detailed letters, noted that Madame de la Sablière, a wealthy and exceptionally cultivated Parisian, drank her tea with milk during the salons she hosted.

The French Revolution put a damper on that—to drink tea was to risk your head—but it came back into fashion half a century later, when all things English became desirable. The oldest Parisian *maisons de thé* ("teahouses") were founded then, such as Mariage Frères in 1854, which today also serves tea-based pastries, including Earl Grey–glazed madeleines that take on the delicate bergamot notes of this flavored black tea.

My rendition is based on Fabrice Le Bourdat's madeleine recipe; he makes perfect ones, bumpy and tender, in his 12th-arrondissement pastry shop.

· NOTES ·
Grind the tea in a mortar with a pestle or use a spice grinder.

To unmold your madeleines like a pro, hold the pan with both hands, tilt it forward so the madeleines face away from you, and bang the side of the pan on a sturdy countertop; the madeleines will pop right out. If your pan is not yet seasoned or you're timid with your banging, it will take a couple more bangs to get them all out.

Freeze the cooled and unglazed madeleines in an airtight container for up to 1 month. Thaw overnight to serve.

· VARIATIONS ·
You can bake the batter as mini-muffins or mini-Bundt cakes.

Try this recipe with any other tea you like.

16 tablespoons (½ pound/225 g) unsalted butter	2 tablespoons finely ground (see Notes) high-quality Earl Grey tea
3 large eggs	1½ teaspoons baking powder
⅔ cup (130 g) sugar	½ teaspoon baking soda
¼ cup (60 ml) milk (any kind)	¼ teaspoon fine sea salt
1½ cups (185 g) all-purpose flour	Orange Glaze (recipe follows)

Prepare the batter the day before serving. Reserve 3 tablespoons of the butter for the pan and, in a small saucepan, melt the remaining butter. In a large bowl, whisk the eggs with the sugar, then whisk in the milk. In a medium bowl, combine the flour, tea, baking powder, baking soda, and salt and stir to remove any lumps. Sprinkle the flour mixture into the wet ingredients, whisking to combine. Whisk the melted butter into the batter. Cover and refrigerate at least overnight, or up to 3 days.

Melt the reserved 3 tablespoons (40 g) butter and use some of it to brush a madeleine pan. Refrigerate for 15 to 30 minutes.

Preheat the oven to 450°F (230°C).

Transfer the batter to a piping bag fitted with a plain ½-inch (1.25 cm) tip. Pipe into the prepared madeleine pan, filling each mold about three-quarters of the way. (If the batter is too stiff, let it come up in temperature for 10 minutes.) Slam the pan once on a sturdy counter to remove any air bubbles. Return the remaining batter to the fridge.

(recipe continues)

Transfer the pan to the oven, immediately reduce the temperature to 350°F (175°C), and bake until the madeleines have a nice bump and are starting to brown around the edges, 15 to 18 minutes. Remove from the oven and unmold immediately (see Notes). Transfer the madeleines to a rack to cool completely. Wash the pan, grease with more of the melted butter, and refrigerate again 15 to 30 minutes before baking a new batch.

Once completely cooled, brush the top of the madeleines (bump side) with the orange glaze. Let set before serving, about 1 hour.

ORANGE GLAZE

Glaçage à l'orange

MAKES
ABOUT ²/₃ CUP
(160 ML)

THIS SIMPLE, TWO-INGREDIENT GLAZE takes all of 1 minute to make, and sets to a thin coating, sweet and tangy, on cakes and cookies. I got the recipe from my mother, who makes it with lemon juice to top her lemon butter cookies (featured in my first cookbook, *Chocolate & Zucchini*). I have used it time and time again to adorn any cake that comes out looking a bit plainer (or, um, darker) than anticipated.

1¼ cups (160 g) powdered sugar

3 to 4 tablespoons (45 to 60 ml) freshly squeezed orange juice (or other citrus juice)

Put the sugar in a bowl and whisk in the orange juice 1 tablespoon at a time, until you get a glaze that is the right consistency for your needs: creamy for butter cookies or a pound cake, a little runnier for madeleines.

Allow your cake or cookies to cool completely before glazing. Use a pastry brush or the back of a spoon to apply it. The glaze will take 30 minutes to 1 hour to set.

I FIRST DISCOVERED GÂTEAU NANTAIS AT CAFÉ TRAMA, A FATHER-AND-daughter bistro close to the Bon Marché department store. I spotted it immediately as I walked in, glowing from the marble counter. An astonishingly moist and fragrant almond cake infused with rum and vanilla, it is crowned by a white glaze that thinly crackles as the spoon digs in.

As the name suggests it hails from Nantes, in the west of France. The city is built on the banks of the Loire River, and became the largest slave port in France in the eighteenth century. (It hasn't been easy for Nantes to come to terms with this dark chapter of its history, but the Quai de la Fosse, where slave ships moored, is now home to a Memorial to the Abolition of Slavery.) The boatloads of riches from the French Caribbean—including sugar, rum, and vanilla—inspired a local *pâtissier* of the time to create this cake.

~GÂTEAU~
nantais

NANTAIS CAKE

SERVES 6 TO 8

10½ tablespoons (150 g) unsalted butter, at room temperature

½ cup (60 g) all-purpose flour

2 cups (200 g) almond flour

½ teaspoon fine sea salt

¾ cup (150 g) sugar

Seeds from 1 small vanilla bean, or 2 teaspoons pure vanilla extract

3 large eggs

3 tablespoons dark rum (or lemon or orange juice)

FOR THE GLAZE

6 tablespoons (45 g) powdered sugar

2 teaspoons dark rum (or lemon or orange juice)

· **NOTE** ·
You can bake the cake the day before serving. Cover with a kitchen towel and glaze just before serving.

Preheat the oven to 350°F (175°C).

Grease an 8-inch (20 cm) round cake pan with ½ teaspoon of the butter and dust the bottom and sides with 1 tablespoon of the all-purpose flour. Tap out the excess.

In a bowl, combine the almond flour, remaining all-purpose flour, and salt. In a medium bowl, combine the remaining butter and the sugar. Add in the vanilla and cream everything together. Whisk in the eggs, one by one, beating well between each addition. Whisk in the rum. Fold the dry ingredients into the wet without overmixing; the batter will be thick.

Pour the batter into the prepared pan and tap it against the counter to settle. Bake until the top of the cake is golden and a cake tester inserted into the center comes out clean, 25 to 30 minutes.

Transfer to a rack and cool in the pan for 20 minutes. Run a knife around the cake to loosen and flip onto a serving plate so the bottom faces up. Cool completely before glazing.

PREPARE THE GLAZE: Put the powdered sugar in a small bowl and stir in the rum. The glaze should be thick and creamy, not runny. Spread on the top of the cooled cake and let set for 1 hour before serving.

THE FRENCH WORD FOR TURNOVER ALSO MEANS 'SLIPPER,' AND WHEN I WAS little, I imagined sliding my feet into these puff pastry pockets, wiggling my toes in the apple compote filling.

As I grew up I fell out of the habit of eating *chaussons*, until I moved into an apartment in the Montmartre neighborhood and discovered that my corner bakery made an old-fashioned one with scalloped edges, a chunky apple filling, and a gorgeous puffed shell studded all over with sugar.

They're easy to make in your own kitchen: a simple apple compote—a mix of apple varieties creates stellar flavor—enclosed in half-moons of puff pastry, homemade or store-bought.

~CHAUSSONS~
aux pommes à l'ancienne

OLD-FASHIONED APPLE TURNOVERS

MAKES 6

1½ pounds (680 g) apples (3 to 4, preferably mixed varieties), peeled, cored, and diced

¼ cup (50 g) granulated sugar

Easy Puff Pastry (page 105), or 12 ounces (340 g) store-bought all-butter puff pastry

Egg wash: 1 large egg lightly beaten with 1 teaspoon water

3 tablespoons (35 g) turbinado sugar, or other raw sugar in coarse crystals

· NOTE ·
If your puff pastry is prerolled and rectangular, cut it into 6 squares. After filling, you'll fold them on the diagonal to make triangular turnovers.

Make the apple compote at least 2 hours before serving. In a medium saucepan, combine the apples and granulated sugar and cook over medium heat, stirring regularly, until soft, 10 to 15 minutes. Crush with a wooden spoon to get a chunky consistency. Increase the heat to medium high and cook, stirring constantly, until the compote leaves a film at the bottom of the pan, 10 more minutes. Remove from the heat and cool completely. Cover and refrigerate for up to 1 day.

Prepare the turnovers at least 1 hour before serving. Line a baking sheet with parchment paper.

Divide the puff pastry into 6 portions (see Note). On a lightly floured work surface, roll out each piece into an oval about 3½ × 4½ inches (9 × 12 cm). Brush one half of each piece of puff pastry with egg wash. Spoon apple compote onto the egg-washed half of each piece without overfilling, leaving a ¾-inch (2 cm) margin. Fold the free dough over the filling, pressing all around to seal.

Transfer the turnovers to the prepared baking sheet, flipping to expose the neater side. Brush again with egg wash. If desired, using the dull side of the tip of a knife, push the dough at intervals along the rounded side, to create scalloped edges. Refrigerate the sheet and the remaining egg wash for 1 hour or overnight.

Preheat the oven to 350°F (175°C).

Brush the turnovers again with egg wash and sprinkle generously with turbinado sugar. Bake until puffy and golden, 30 to 35 minutes. Transfer to a rack to cool. Serve slightly warm or at room temperature. The texture is best on the day they are made.

~FLAN~
parisien

PARISIAN FLAN

SERVES 8 TO 10

MANY PARISIANS CITE THE FLAN AS A CHILDHOOD FAVORITE AND SEEK IT out at every *boulangerie* they visit, comparing notes with other aficionados on the crispness of the crust and the creaminess of the filling. Once you know to look for it, you will spot the high-walled vanilla custard tart everywhere in the city, precut into generous slices. Your teeth sink into the fresh, jiggly filling, hitting the flaky crust and shooting messages of delight to your brain.

Making your own is a three-step process, but it's not difficult: You'll prepare the vanilla custard first, cool it, then fill the crust and bake until the top is darkly spotted.

· NOTES ·

You can also flavor the flan with vanilla seeds: Split a vanilla bean lengthwise and scrape the seeds into the milk in the saucepan. Add the vanilla pod, too, then bring to a simmer. Remove the pod before pouring the milk into the egg mixture.

The flan keeps in the refrigerator for 2 to 3 days.

2½ cups (600 ml) whole milk

¾ cup (150 g) sugar

⅔ cup (70 g) cornstarch

3 large eggs

2 teaspoons pure vanilla extract (see Note)

⅔ cup (160 ml) heavy cream

1 tablespoon unsalted butter, for greasing

Tart Pastry (page 86) with 3 tablespoons (35 g) sugar added with the flour

Prepare the filling 5 to 8 hours before serving. In a medium saucepan, combine the milk and 6 tablespoons (75 g) of the sugar and bring to a simmer. In a large bowl, combine the cornstarch with the remaining 6 tablespoons (75 g) sugar. Add the eggs and vanilla and whisk until smooth. Whisk in the cream and the simmering milk, little by little.

Pour the mixture back into the saucepan and return to medium heat. Bring to a simmer, whisking as the custard thickens, about 4 minutes. It is ready when the whisk leaves clear traces, and will continue to thicken as it cools. Pour the custard into a baking dish or other large vessel, cover, and cool to room temperature, about 2 hours.

Grease a 10-inch (25 cm) springform pan or cake pan that is 2 inches (5 cm) deep with the butter.

Roll out the tart pastry to a thickness of about ⅛ inch (3 mm) and line the pan with it, running the rolling pin over the pan edges to trim. Put the pastry in the freezer for at least 1 to 2 hours. (Or if making ahead, cover with plastic wrap and store in the freezer for up to 1 month.)

Preheat the oven to 400°F (200°C).

Whisk the custard to break it up, pour into the frozen tart shell, and smooth the surface with a spatula. Bake for 25 minutes, then increase the temperature to 450°F (230°C) and bake another 10 minutes, watching closely, until the top of the flan has dark brown spots. If you find the exposed sides of the crust are browning too quickly, drape loosely with strips of foil.

Cool the flan for 1 hour, then refrigerate until cold, about 1½ hours.

CHOCOLATE ICE CREAM
WITH NUTS & RAISINS

SERVES 6

THE IMPOSSIBLY CHARMING ÎLE SAINT-LOUIS IS A TINY ISLAND IN THE SEINE, just five blocks by two, right in the center of Paris. In fair weather, an afternoon stroll along the seventeenth-century streets must end with a scoop of artisanal ice cream from Berthillon (see page 128) eaten on the banks of the river; it's almost an obligation. Although Berthillon offers, on any given day, a good thirty flavors, I confess my brain only processes the chocolate ones, of which there are several. And if the *glace chocolat mendiant* is up there, I do a happy dance.

This is a killer chocolate ice cream, deep and smooth, with raisins, toasted hazelnuts and walnuts mixed in, so every bite is creamy, crunchy, and chewy all at the same time. It is a nod to the popular chocolate confection of the same name, a thin disk of chocolate studded with nuts and dried fruits.

Berthillon does not divulge recipes—believe me, I tried—so I built my version on the classic *crème glacée* method shared by Martine Lambert, another fine ice-cream artisan who is based in Normandy and has a couple of shops in Paris. It is easy to prepare, even without an ice-cream maker, and will make you very, very popular.

· NOTES ·

No ice-cream maker? No problem! Put the container of chilled mixture in the freezer and stir every hour or so, scraping the sides in toward the center, until the ice cream is completely set, 4 to 5 hours. Stir in the nuts and raisins when the ice cream is almost done.

Instead of turning the preparation into ice cream, you can serve it like chocolate pudding after the overnight refrigeration.

Homemade ice cream without additives tends to become very hard in the freezer overnight. I like to form individual scoops right after churning, freeze them on a baking sheet lined with parchment paper, then transfer to a larger container for an easy after-dinner treat.

· VARIATION ·

Substitute other nuts and dried fruits as preferred.

4 large egg yolks

½ cup (100 g) sugar

1⅔ cups (400 ml) milk (any kind)

7 ounces (200 g) high-quality bittersweet chocolate (60 to 70% cacao), very finely chopped

¼ cup (25 g) walnut halves, toasted and roughly chopped

¼ cup (30 g) hazelnuts, toasted and roughly chopped

¼ cup (40 g) dark raisins

Prepare the chocolate custard the day before serving. Create a double boiler. In a medium saucepan, bring about 2 inches (5 cm) of water to a simmer. Choose a medium, heatproof bowl that will fit over the pan without touching the water below (pour out some of the water if needed).

In the heatproof bowl, but on your counter, whisk the egg yolks and sugar together until smooth and doubled in volume. Whisk in the milk. Put the bowl over the saucepan of simmering water and whisk constantly as the mixture heats up to 185°F (85°C); this will take about 10 minutes. Remove the pan from the heat.

Add the chocolate, let sit for 1 minute, then whisk until melted and smooth. Cool to room temperature, then cover and refrigerate overnight. It will be very thick.

Churn in an ice-cream maker according to the manufacturer's instructions, adding the walnuts, hazelnuts, and raisins in the final minute of churning to incorporate.

Serve immediately, or store in an airtight container in the freezer.

LA MAISON BERTHILLON

≡Three Generations of Ice-Cream Artisans≡

"WHAT WOULD PAPY DO?" IS THE PHRASE LIONEL CHAUVIN COULD GET tattooed on his wrist.

A third-generation ice-cream maker in his late thirties, he constantly measures up the quality of his production to that of his late grandfather, Raymond Berthillon, who started making frozen treats on Paris's Île Saint-Louis in 1954.

Sorbets had fallen out of style back then and he was the one to reintroduce them, using only the best in-season fruit to deliver the essence of their flavor, concentrated in a single scoop. He was just as intent on making superior ice cream, going out at dawn to snatch the freshest ingredients at the food market of Les Halles, across the Seine.

He was soon Paris's favorite *glacier*, forming partnerships with restaurants around the city who climbed over one another to serve the good stuff, and making Maison Berthillon as obligatory a stop for visitors as the Louvre or Notre-Dame. (During the month of August, when Parisians leave the city, the storied boutique is closed for its annual break. But other retailers on the Île continue to sell Berthillon ice cream.)

Raymond Berthillon was initially running the operation with his mother-in-law and his wife; he passed it on to his daughter and son-in-law, who in turn involved their son and daughter, Lionel and Muriel. It's a flourishing family business that maintains its old-school vibe and purist approach (fresh ingredients, no additives of any kind) yet comes up with new and inventive recipes monthly—*le parfum du mois* that fans live for—and modernizes processes to stay on top of the game.

The small manufacturing lab on rue Saint-Louis-en-l'Île churns out one thousand quarts of ice creams and sorbets daily, in thirty flavors—from a total repertoire of ninety. The recipes are not fixed; they have to be adjusted daily to the nature of the ingredients the team is working with, and no ice cream goes out without being green-lighted by a member of the Berthillon family.

The *fraise des bois* (wild strawberry) sorbet is legendary, as is the *marron glacé* (candied chestnut) ice cream; as for me, I would sell my soul for any of the half-dozen chocolate flavors they offer, especially the extra-bitter cacao sorbet and the Chocolate Ice Cream with Nuts and Raisins (page 126).

PARISIANS TYPICALLY LIVE IN SMALL APARTMENTS, AND FOR THOSE OF US with young children, on weekends it is vital to find activities that get everyone out of the house before cabin fever sets in. Fortunately, Paris is full of parks—and carousels. The old-fashioned ones with horses and carriages are the most attractive, but children prefer the garish ones with motorcycles and helicopters painted with images of Bart Simpson and Super Mario.

Aesthetics aside, the universal draw of the carousel is the snack stand that leans against it, coloring the air with the sweet scents of warm crêpes and waffles. These are the same kind of waffles you will find at fairs all around the country: crisp on the outside, light and soft on the inside, steaming hot in the cold winter air. All kinds of messy toppings are offered—whipped cream! chocolate sauce! chestnut cream!—but I favor the simple sprinkling of powdered sugar that makes children sneeze and leaves the tips of their noses white.

2⅓ cups (300 g)
all-purpose flour

1 tablespoon baking powder

½ teaspoon fine sea salt

⅓ cup (70 g) sugar

½ cup (110 g) butter,
melted and cooled

2 large eggs

2 cups (480 ml) milk
(any kind)

FOR SERVING (OPTIONAL)

Powdered sugar

Simple Chocolate Sauce
(page 247)

Chantilly Whipped Cream
(page 143)

Sweetened chestnut cream
(available from gourmet markets
and specialty foods stores)

Maple syrup

Chocolate shavings

· NOTES ·

The batter can be cooked in a skillet to make excellent pancakes.

Leftover waffles reheat well in the toaster or toaster oven.

In a bowl, combine the flour, baking powder, salt, and sugar. Make a well in the center and add the melted butter and eggs. Whisk to combine with part of the flour. Pour in the milk slowly as you whisk to get a smooth batter (a few lumps are fine). It will resemble pancake batter.

Cover and refrigerate 1 hour. (The batter will keep for up to 2 days but gives best results after 1 hour.) Whisk again before using.

Preheat your waffle iron and grease it if necessary.

Pour in the batter using a small ladle. Each waffle mold should be filled enough that the waffle will rise to meet the top, but not so much that the dough will overflow. Cook until golden brown, 5 to 6 minutes; the steam escaping from the iron will lessen significantly when the waffles are almost ready. (Avoid opening the iron too early or your waffles will split apart.)

Let stand for 2 minutes on a rack before serving. Serve with powdered sugar, chocolate sauce, whipped cream, chestnut cream, maple syrup, chocolate shavings, or whatever else you desire.

~MAKROUTS~
au four

BAKED
MAKROUTS

MAKES ABOUT 48 MAKROUTS

WHEN THE CITY GETS BOILING HOT IN THE SUMMER, I ESCAPE TO THE GREAT Mosque of Paris in the 5th arrondissement. In the shaded courtyard, I sip hot mint tea and pretend I am in a hidden riad in Marrakech, amid fountains and cool mosaic tiling.

The first and largest mosque ever built in France, it was inaugurated in the 1920s to honor the French Arab soldiers fallen during World War I. While it is primarily a place of worship, it also functions as a restaurant and a hammam for visitors of any faith. At the tea salon, you can pick out a North African pastry from the cornucopian display. I like the *makrout*, an orange blossom semolina cake filled with a date paste. The traditional version is fried, but our baby-sitter once brought baked makrouts her mother had made, and I asked if she would teach me her recipe.

· NOTE ·

Semolina flour is made from hard durum wheat; you will find it at specialty food stores and Middle Eastern markets. To get the makrout's signature nubby texture, use the two kinds listed—one fine and one medium—if you can; if not, use only the fine grind.

1⅓ cups (250 g) fine-grind semolina flour, plus more for dusting

1⅓ cups (250 g) medium-grind semolina

2 tablespoons (25 g) sugar

½ teaspoon ground cinnamon

10½ tablespoons (150 g) unsalted butter, melted

12 medium (8 ounces/225 g) soft Medjool dates, pitted, or 7 ounces/ 200 g ready-made date paste

2 teaspoons olive oil

4 tablespoons (60 ml) orange blossom water

FOR THE GLAZE (OPTIONAL)

½ cup (120 ml) honey

2 tablespoons orange blossom water

In a medium bowl, combine the semolinas, sugar, and cinnamon. Add the melted butter and mix with the tips of your fingers. Let stand for 30 minutes. In a separate bowl, mash the dates with the olive oil and 1 tablespoon of the orange blossom water to get a smooth paste. (If the dates are too thick, use scissors or two knives to shred them before mashing.)

Add the remaining 3 tablespoons orange blossom water to the semolina mixture and rub with your fingers. Stir in ½ cup (120 ml) cold water. Then start adding water 1 tablespoon at a time, kneading it in as you go, just until the dough comes together. It should be smooth as a baby's bottom, and lightly clammy.

Preheat the oven to 350°F (175°C) and line a baking sheet with parchment paper or a silicone baking mat.

Lightly dust your work surface with semolina flour. Divide the dough into 4 portions. Roll one portion into a log about 12 inches (30 cm) long. Press a lengthwise groove down the center of the log and shape the sides into "walls" about 1½ inches (4 cm) high on either side of the groove. Spread one-quarter of the date paste in the groove and close the walls over it, pressing to seal. Flip the log and pinch together any cracks on the surface.

Use the dull side of a knife to decorate the log with lines at a diagonal. Cut the log into diamond-shaped pieces about 1 inch (2.5 cm) wide. Arrange on the prepared baking sheet about 1 inch (2.5 cm) apart.

Repeat with the remaining dough and date paste.

Bake until golden, 15 to 20 minutes. Cool completely on the sheet before glazing, if desired.

GLAZE THE MAKROUTS: Set a rack over a tray. In a small saucepan, melt the honey over low heat. Stir in the orange blossom water. Using chopsticks, dip the makrouts on both sides into the syrup and put on the rack. Let set for at least 3 hours or overnight.

ANGELINA, THE ICONIC PARISIAN TEAROOM, IS FAMOUS FOR ITS VELVETY hot chocolate (page 142) and their signature pastry, the Mont-Blanc. Named after the highest mountain in the Alps, this dome-like construction of meringue and whipped cream is topped with thinly piped "vermicelli" of sweet chestnut cream. It's a heavenly mix of textures—crunchy, airy, creamy—and the nutty flavor of chestnuts is irresistible.

The classic mountain shape is difficult to make at home; it quickly turns into a toppling mess. Not wanting to get too technical, I played around with different ways to serve it: It works well in alternating layers in a cup or glass, but the winning format was suggested by my dear friend Laurence, who dropped by on a recipe-testing day. Together we made long rectangular Mont-Blancs to be divided into servings, and this is what I recommend.

~MONT-BLANC~

CHESTNUT CREAM MERINGUE

SERVES 6 TO 8

FOR THE MERINGUE

3 tablespoons (40 g) granulated sugar

¼ cup (40 g) powdered sugar

3 large egg whites, at room temperature

¼ teaspoon cream of tartar

¼ teaspoon fine sea salt

FOR ASSEMBLING

1 cup (240 ml) heavy cream, chilled

1 cup (250 g) sweetened chestnut cream (available from gourmet markets and specialty foods stores), chilled

· NOTE ·

In humid weather, the meringues may absorb the ambient moisture and go soft. Under those circumstances, it's best to bake the meringues as close to serving time as possible.

PREPARE THE MERINGUE 4 HOURS BEFORE SERVING: Position racks at the upper and lower thirds, preheat the oven to 225°F (100°C), and line 2 baking sheets with parchment paper.

In a small bowl, combine the granulated sugar and powdered sugar.

In the bowl of a stand mixer fitted with the whisk attachment, combine the egg whites, cream of tartar, and salt. Beat the egg whites on low and then medium speed, until they form medium peaks. Whisk in one-third of the sugar mixture and continue beating on medium speed as you sprinkle in the remaining sugar, a little bit at a time. The meringue is ready when it is glossy and forms stiff peaks; this will take about 10 minutes.

Transfer it to a piping bag fitted with a ½-inch (1.25 cm) plain or star tip. Working in a tight zigzag, pipe the meringue onto one of the baking sheets to form 4 long rectangles about 1½ × 12 inches (4 × 30 cm). Pipe the rest of the meringue into 1-inch (2.5 cm) dots on the second baking sheet; you should have enough to make about 60. (You won't be needing them for this recipe; when baked, serve with coffee or ice cream.)

(recipe continues)

Bake until the meringues are completely set and detach from the parchment paper easily, 1½ to 2 hours, switching the positions of the sheets top to bottom and back to front halfway through. If the meringues begin to color, reduce the oven temperature slightly.

While the meringues are baking, clean the piping bag and tip. Clean the mixer bowl and whisk and put in the fridge to chill.

Remove the meringue rectangles carefully from the parchment paper and cool on a rack.

FOR THE ASSEMBLY: Put the chilled heavy cream in the chilled mixer bowl. Snap on the whisk attachment and start whisking the cream on medium-low speed, then increase the speed slightly every 30 seconds or so, until the whisk leaves clear traces in the cream and the cream forms beautiful, firm peaks when you lift up the whisk, 4 to 5 minutes total. Transfer to the piping bag fitted with the tip you used for the meringue.

Just before serving, spoon the chestnut cream into a sturdy sandwich bag and chase out the air as you close it. Snip a tiny (1 mm) opening in one corner; this will be your "vermicelli" piping bag.

Arrange the 4 rectangles of meringue on a serving dish large enough to accommodate them. Pipe whipped cream along the length of each meringue. Working your way from one end of a rectangle to the other, pipe vermicelli of chestnut cream in a tight side-to-side movement to conceal the meringue and whipped cream.

Bring whole to the table and slice into thirds or quarters depending on appetite.

PARIS IS A CITY EQUALLY SMITTEN WITH FOOD AND FASHION, AND IT adopts the latest health trends with enthusiasm. This is how cold-pressed juices entered the gastronomic landscape in the early teens, promising vibrant flavor and a boost of micronutrients in a single glass.

Some outlets are more exacting than others about quality and freshness, and one of the best providers I know is Nubio, a small company run with passion and style by two young women on the hip rue Paul-Bert. One of my favorites is the *Petite Douceur* ("small treat"), a bottle of almond milk flavored with dates and vanilla. Nubio makes it with almond milk they press daily in a dedicated extractor, but in a pinch I prepare my own using almond butter, which I always have on hand, and mix it in the blender. This drink is silky, lightly sweet, and full of flavor: the perfect pick-me-up in the middle of the afternoon and a great base for smoothies.

~LAIT D'AMANDE~
aux dates et à la vanille

ALMOND MILK
WITH DATES & VANILLA

SERVES 2 TO 4

3 tablespoons (50 g) smooth all-natural almond butter, preferably raw

3 Medjool dates (about 2 ounces/60 g total), pitted and chopped

½ teaspoon pure vanilla extract

A pinch of sea salt

3 ice cubes

2 cups (480 ml) filtered water

· **VARIATIONS** ·
Add a handful of berries or a pinch of cinnamon, or use another type of nut butter.

In a blender, combine the almond butter, dates, vanilla, salt, ice, and water. Process on high speed until completely smooth, 20 to 30 seconds.

Pour into glasses and serve immediately, or refrigerate up to a day (shake well before drinking).

LA MAISON CLUIZEL

≡Three Generations of Chocolatiers≡

RUE SAINT-HONORÉ IS A LONG AND ELEGANT STREET THAT RUNS ACROSS the 1st arrondissement, from the Madeleine church to Les Halles, a strip of chic where some of the most exclusive brands have stores. The street happens to be named after the patron saint of bakers, and it is where the great classic of French pastry, the Saint-Honoré—a gorgeous construction of caramel-topped cream puffs and meringue-lightened pastry cream—was invented in 1850.

It is in this environment of sweetness and luxury that the Cluizel family established its first Paris boutique to sell the bean-to-bar chocolates they've been manufacturing for more than sixty years.

There are only about two dozen artisans in France who make chocolate from the bean, an elaborate process that involves a set of dedicated machines that roast, crush, sort, grind, blend, and conche, turning the fermented and dried cacao beans into what we think of as chocolate. The vast majority buy the finished product from specialized manufacturers, to melt and use as needed to create their chocolate-based confections.

The Cluizel story first began with Marcelle and Marc Cluizel in 1948; they were soon joined by their fifteen-year-old son, Michel, who eventually took over and continued to improve on the manufacturing process—most of the machines they use were custom-designed to the family's specifications—and his vision allowed the company to develop internationally.

Now run by Michel's own children, Marc, Sylvie, and Catherine, the company distributes chocolate bars and confections to individuals and professionals in more than fifty countries. Yet many of the steps in the process continue to be done by hand, and the company is committed to sustainable practices and quality ingredients, using only pure cacao butter, whole-bean vanilla, and no flavorings in their chocolates.

The French language had no term to designate a bean-to-bar chocolatier, so Michel Cluizel coined and trademarked *cacaofèvier* (*fève de cacao* means "cacao bean"). Central to the Cluizel approach are the direct, fair-trade partnerships they've established with five cacao plantations, in Madagascar, Mexico, the Dominican Republic, São Tomé and Principe, and Papua New Guinea. The quality of these relationships is reflected in my favorite of the Cluizels' signature products: a line of single-plantation bars that express the individuality of each terroir, like grand cru wines.

~CHOCOLAT CHAUD~
parisien

PARISIAN
HOT
CHOCOLATE

SERVES 6

TO WARD OFF THE BITTER WINTER COLD, PARISIANS FLOCK TO CAFÉ patios, wrap themselves in the blankets provided, and ask their server for a *chocolat chaud*. Presented with an optional small cup of whipped cream, it is served in a *chocolatière* (hot chocolate pot) that gets them a good two cupfuls of the velvety chocolate drink.

The quality of chocolate used will make or break hot chocolate. Well-known spots like Café de Flore, Les Deux Magots, and Angelina retain their historic aura, certainly, and their thick chocolat chaud won't disappoint. But Parisians in the know favor the ones offered by master chocolatiers such as Jacques Genin or Jean-Paul Hévin.

Make it in the comfort of your own home and you'll be able to dunk the tip of a croissant into your cup, as French kids do for *le goûter*.

· NOTE ·
For extra flavor, infuse the milk with a vanilla bean the day before. Split the bean open; scrape the seeds into the milk and add the pod, too. Bring the milk to a simmer, then let cool completely. Refrigerate overnight in an airtight container and strain out the pod before using.

¼ cup (50 g) sugar

3 cups (720 ml) milk (any kind)

8 ounces (230 g) bittersweet chocolate (60 to 70% cacao), finely chopped

Chantilly Whipped Cream (opposite), for serving

In a medium saucepan, heat the sugar over medium heat until it melts and turns amber, without stirring; simply tilt the pan from time to time to encourage even caramelization. This should take 4 to 5 minutes. Remove from the heat to cool for 1 minute.

Carefully pour in the milk, return to medium heat, and bring to a simmer, stirring well to dissolve. Reduce the heat to medium low. Whisk in the chocolate and stir until melted. Bring to a low simmer and cook, stirring continually without allowing the mixture to boil, until the hot chocolate is thickened, 5 to 8 minutes longer. (You can make this in advance; cool and gently reheat before serving.)

Pour into cups and let rest 5 minutes. Serve with Chantilly cream, either in a bowl on the side or piped onto the surface of the hot chocolate at the last minute using a piping bag fitted with a star tip.

CHANTILLY WHIPPED CREAM

Crème Chantilly

MAKES
1½ CUPS
(360 ML)

THIS SWEETENED WHIPPED CREAM is a staple of French *pâtisserie*. It is named after Chantilly château, a short train ride outside of Paris, where some believe it was invented by chef François Vatel in the seventeenth century. Use it to instantly elevate a salad of seasonal berries, a cup of ice cream (page 246), a simple slice of cake, or a crêpe with chocolate sauce (page 247).

⅔ cup (160 ml) heavy cream, chilled

2 tablespoons (12 g) powdered sugar

½ vanilla bean

If possible, chill a medium bowl and the whisk attachment of an electric mixer in the refrigerator 2 hours before you begin.

In the chilled bowl, combine the chilled heavy cream and powdered sugar. Scrape the vanilla seeds out of the vanilla bean into the bowl. Using the electric mixer, start whisking the cream on medium-low speed, then increase the speed slightly every 30 seconds or so to reach medium-high speed. It is ready when the whisk leaves clear traces and the cream forms beautiful, firm peaks when you lift up the whisk, 4 to 5 minutes total.

Transfer to a container with a tight-fitting lid (or a piping bag fitted with a plain or star tip) and chill for 2 hours or overnight before using.

MANY PASTRIES FILL THE GLASS CASES AT THE ORIGINAL LADURÉE SHOP on rue Royale, yet it is the smooth, pastel-colored macarons that attract shoppers, beckoning them to buy just one, maybe two, oh, sure, why not a box of eight?

The Parisian macaron, a sandwich of two almond meringue cookies assembled around a ganache filling, appeared around 1830 and was indeed popularized by Ladurée. Nowadays they are sold everywhere, lined up in color-coordinated rows. Best to do a bit of research before you buy them, though: Few bakeries have the time and resources to make their own, and many sell factory-made ones to cash in on the trend.

In evoking modern macaron history, we must acknowledge the contribution of pastry chef Pierre Hermé, who left Ladurée to start his own pastry shop in the late nineties. He soon expanded his range of flavors to include such innovative notes as dogwood, olive oil, or white truffle, drawing the macaron away from its classic background of chocolate, raspberry, caramel, and pistachio.

The French passion for macarons doesn't seem to wane, and I'm happy to report that these naturally gluten-free treats are within reach of the home baker. You may not achieve Hermé-level perfection on your first try, but still you'll marvel at your creations.

~MACARONS~
au chocolat tout simples

SIMPLE CHOCOLATE MACARONS

MAKES ABOUT 30 MACARONS

FOR THE MACARON SHELLS

1 cup (100 g) almond flour, the finest grind you can find (see Notes)

3 tablespoons (15 g) unsweetened Dutch-process cocoa powder

3 large egg whites

¼ teaspoon fine sea salt

⅛ teaspoon cream of tartar

¼ cup (50 g) granulated sugar

1⅓ cups (150 g) powdered sugar

FOR THE GANACHE FILLING

4 ounces (115 g) high-quality bittersweet chocolate (60 to 70% cacao), finely chopped

⅓ cup (80 ml) heavy cream

1 tablespoon (15 g) unsalted butter, diced

· NOTES ·

If the almond flour you find is a little coarse, grind it to a finer consistency in a food processor, working in short pulses. (This does not work in a blender.)

If you don't have a piping bag, use a sturdy freezer bag with one corner snipped off.

MAKE THE MACARON SHELLS: Position your oven racks at the upper and lower thirds, preheat the oven to 325°F (165°C), and line two baking sheets with parchment paper or silicone baking mats. Make sure that the baking sheets and mats are dry.

Sift the almond flour and cocoa powder into a bowl. Discard the coarse almond pieces that don't make it through.

(recipe continues)

In a medium bowl, with a hand mixer, whisk the egg whites with the salt and cream of tartar on low speed until foamy, about 30 seconds. Increase the speed to medium high and beat until they form medium-soft peaks, about 1 minute. Continuing to beat on medium-high speed, sprinkle in the granulated sugar in 4 to 5 additions, counting 15 seconds between each, and whisk to stiff peaks. The meringue should be glossy and white. Keep beating on medium-high speed slowly adding the powdered sugar, until you reach the stiff-peak stage again.

Fold in the sifted almonds and cocoa in a circular, vertical motion to avoid deflating and overbeating. When you lift the spatula, the batter should drip from it in a ribbon.

Scoop the macaron batter into a piping bag fitted with a plain ½-inch (1.25 cm) tip and, holding the bag vertically above the baking sheet, form 1½-inch (4 cm) rounds about 1½ inches (4 cm) apart. You should have about 30 per sheet. Slam the baking sheets several times on the counter to remove air bubbles.

Bake until the macarons are domed, 12 to 16 minutes, switching the positions of the sheets top to bottom and back to front after 10 minutes. To test for doneness, try wiggling a few shells side to side gently. If they wiggle from the base, they need a little more baking. If they don't budge, they are done.

Cool for a few minutes on the sheets, then gently lift and transfer to a rack to cool completely.

PREPARE THE GANACHE FILLING: Put the chopped chocolate in a medium heatproof bowl.

In a small saucepan, bring the cream to a boil. Pour over the chocolate and stir (without beating) with a spatula until smooth and shiny. Add the butter and stir until incorporated.

Clean the piping bag and tip and scoop the ganache into it. Cool for 30 minutes.

To assemble, pair together the macaron shells closest in size. Pipe a dollop of ganache, about 1 rounded teaspoon, on one shell in each pair. Put the matching shell on top, press and twist gently to even out the filling. Refrigerate for at least 2 hours to set, or overnight.

~MINI-PAVÉS~
garnis

STUFFED
BREAD
ROLLS

MAKES 6 ROLLS

IN BAKERIES, THE TERM *PAVÉ* **(LITERALLY, PAVING STONE) IS USED FOR** loaves of artisanal bread shaped like rough squares. Miniature *pavés garnis* adopt the same squarish shape, with tasty fillings folded into the dough: strips of ham or bacon, cubes of cheese, chopped olives, walnuts, on their own or in combination.

They're the perfect afternoon snack if you're in the mood for something savory to tide you over until dinner. They are easy to make at home and will feel deliciously fancy as part of a brunch spread or as a complement to a simple salad lunch. In the recipe below I suggest an assortment with olives, bacon, and cheese, but you can try other fillings, or make an "everything" batch so every bite is different.

FOR THE FERMENTED DOUGH

½ teaspoon active dry yeast

⅓ cup (80 ml) lukewarm water

4½ ounces (130 g) all-purpose flour (about 1 cup)

½ teaspoon fine sea salt

FOR THE FINAL DOUGH

7 ounces (200 g) all-purpose flour (about 1½ cups), plus more for dusting

½ teaspoon active dry yeast

½ teaspoon fine sea salt

⅔ cup (160 ml) lukewarm water

FOR THE FILLING

3½ slices (3½ ounces/100 g) thick-cut bacon, sliced into thin strips to make lardons (see Note, page 61)

¼ cup (45 g) black olives, pitted and chopped

1½ ounces (45 g) hard cheese, such as Comté, medium diced

Olive oil, for brushing

· NOTE ·
The cooled rolls can be frozen. Thaw overnight on the counter and return to a 400°F (200°C) oven for 5 minutes to revive the texture.

MAKE THE FERMENTED DOUGH THE DAY BEFORE SERVING: Proof the yeast in the ⅓ cup lukewarm water (see How to Proof Yeast, page 21).

In a medium bowl, using a wooden spoon or dough whisk, mix the flour with the yeast mixture and salt until the dough comes together. Cover the bowl with plastic wrap and let stand at room temperature for 1 to 2 hours. Refrigerate overnight.

MAKE THE FINAL DOUGH: Remove the fermented dough from the refrigerator 1 hour before continuing. Add the flour, yeast, salt, and lukewarm water. Mix with a wooden spoon until incorporated. The dough will be fairly loose and sticky. Cover and let stand for 1 hour at room temperature in a draft-free spot.

"Fold" the dough onto itself by slipping a flexible spatula between the dough and the side of the bowl, pulling the dough up and over itself, and working your way all around the bowl in this fashion. Cover and let stand again for 1 hour at room temperature in a draft-free spot.

FILL THE DOUGH: In a small skillet, cook the bacon over medium-low heat until browned. Scoop out into a bowl. (Save the rendered fat for another use.)

Line a baking sheet with parchment paper and put the 3 fillings (bacon, olives, cheese) in separate cups.

Scrape the dough onto a floured work surface and divide into 6 equal pieces. Working with one piece at a time, flatten to a thickness of about ⅓ inch (1 cm). Sprinkle with half of one of the fillings and roll the dough up tightly, tucking in the sides to form squarish rolls. Put seam side down on the baking sheet. Repeat with the remaining dough and fillings: You should have 2 bacon rolls, 2 cheese rolls, and 2 olive rolls. Cover loosely with a kitchen towel and let rest for 30 minutes at room temperature in a draft-free spot.

Put a baking dish on the lowest rack of the oven and fill it with boiling water. If you have a pizza stone, put it on the lower middle rack of the oven. Preheat the oven to 450°F (230°C).

Dust off any excess flour from the tops of the rolls and brush them with olive oil. Transfer the baking sheet to the center rack, or, if using a pizza stone, slide the parchment paper onto it carefully, using a pizza peel if possible. Bake for 10 minutes, then reduce the oven temperature to 400°F (200°C) and bake until golden brown, about 20 minutes more.

Transfer to a rack to cool completely before serving.

~KOUIGN AMANN~

SALTED CARAMEL
FLAKY PIE

SERVES 10

ONE OF MY FONDEST FOOD MEMORIES FROM CHILDHOOD COMES FROM spending vacations in Brittany and eating *kouign amann* from a little stand at the local market. Pronounced queen-ya-MAHN, meaning "butter cake" in the Breton language, this is an irresistibly buttery, caramelized pastry created in 1860 in Douarnenez, a small coastal town in Brittany.

For years, it was impossible to find in Paris, but now bakers have caught on and added it to their roster of treats. I love to make it myself, too. It is a surefire way to delight my friends when they come over for an afternoon tea.

The process is similar to that of making Easy Puff Pastry (page 105): The yeasted bread dough is folded over butter and sugar and bakes into a marvelous laminated pie-meets-bread crusted with buttery caramel.

½ teaspoon active dry yeast

⅔ cup (160 ml) lukewarm water

12 tablespoons (170 g) unsalted butter, cold

⅔ cup (130 g) sugar

1¾ cups (230 g) all-purpose flour

½ teaspoon fine sea salt

1 tablespoon milk (any kind)

At least 2½ hours before serving, proof the yeast in the lukewarm water (see How to Proof Yeast, page 21).

In the meantime, grease a 10-inch (25 cm) cake pan (not springform) with 1 tablespoon (15 g) of the butter and sprinkle with 2 tablespoons (25 g) of the sugar.

In a large mixing bowl, combine the flour and salt. Form a well in the center and pour in the yeast mixture. Mix with a wooden spoon or dough whisk until incorporated. On a clean work surface, knead the dough for 5 minutes, until smooth and springy. Let rest for 5 minutes.

In the meantime, put the remaining butter between two sheets of parchment paper and bang it with your fist to flatten into a 7-inch (17 cm) round.

Flour your work surface lightly, and roll out the dough to form an 8-inch (20 cm) round. Put the round of butter on top of the round of dough and pour the sugar over the butter. Fold the bottom third up toward the center, like a letter, and press with the tips of your fingers to seal. Fold the top third down and over, making sure the layer of dough encapsulates the butter and sugar and press to seal. Fold both sides in to meet in the center, making sure again that the butter and sugar are trapped inside, and press to seal. Put on a plate and refrigerate for 15 minutes.

(recipe continues)

Flour your work surface lightly again. Roll the dough out to form a rectangle about 8 × 12 inches (20 × 30 cm). Fold in three like a letter. Give the dough a quarter turn, roll it out into a rectangle about 5 × 15 inches (13 × 38 cm), and fold in three again, ending with a 5-inch (13 cm) square. Fold the four corners of the square in to meet in the center, flip, and tuck the edges under to shape into a ball. Return to the fridge for 15 minutes.

Preheat the oven to 400°F (200°C).

Flour your work surface lightly again. Roll the dough out into a 10-inch (25 cm) round, and transfer to the prepared pan. Brush with the milk and, using the tip of a sharp knife, score the top in a shallow crisscross pattern. Bake until golden brown, 30 to 40 minutes. Using a spoon, scoop some of the melted butter that pools on the sides and baste the top.

Let cool in the pan for 15 minutes, then lift with a spatula and transfer to a serving plate. (If the caramel has already set in the pan, pop it back into the oven for 5 minutes.) Serve slightly warm or at room temperature. It tastes best the day it is made; leftovers can be reheated for 5 minutes in a 400°F (200°C) oven.

EARLY EVENING

L'APÉRO

Parmi la foule des grands boulevards
Quelle joie inouïe
D'aller ainsi au hasard
—CHARLES TRENET

IF I HAD TO NAME A SINGLE CUSTOM THAT EPITOMIZES the French approach to life, and the enjoyment thereof, it would be *l'apéro*, short for *l'apéritif*.

On the surface, it is simply a predinner drink shared with friends over a few bites. But really, it is time stolen from the rush of modern life, when you gather at a bar or café and debrief from your day, discuss world events, joke around, and unwind. I am always uplifted by the tangle of long legs crowding under tiny sidewalk tables, the misty glasses of white wine clinking, and the waiters hurriedly slicing baguettes and *saucissons* to keep up with orders.

Despite living in small abodes, Parisians have a strong culture of hosting friends; nothing strengthens relationships like inviting people into your home. Having them over for the apéritif before going out to dinner is the most informal way to do so, one that's easy to improvise at the last moment and is a great fit for new acquaintances and old friends alike. Drinks and nibbles will be consumed, and after an hour or two the party will move on, happy and rejuvenated from the lively conversation.

Apéritif food is meant to be simple, and it is fine to offer store-bought items so long as they've been chosen with care from the charcuterie or fine-foods shop. The well-prepared host keeps a few jarred terrines and spreads in the pantry just for such occasions. If you want to get cooking, however, the following recipes are easily eaten while standing and holding a glass of wine or a freshly shaken cocktail.

~TERRINE~
de poulet à la pistache

CHICKEN & PISTACHIO
TERRINE

SERVES 8 TO 10

I KEEP JARRED SPREADS ON HAND TO SERVE TO LAST-MINUTE *APÉRITIF* guests; all I need to do is pick up a fresh baguette from the bakery around the corner. But if I've had some advance warning, I delight in preparing meat terrines from scratch: Most people buy these ready-made at the charcuterie, so making your own never fails to impress. I love this chicken and pistachio recipe for its lightness, ease of preparation, and big flavor.

Following the example of La Régalade, a popular gastro-bistro in the 14th arrondissement where diners are greeted with a generous country terrine passed around from table to table, I serve it straight from the earthenware dish, with a knife planted in the middle, and offer thick slices of crusty bread and cornichons to go with it.

3 ounces (85 g) day-old bread, diced

2 tablespoons milk (any kind)

2 tablespoons Cognac or other brandy (substitute the same amount of milk if preferred)

1 pound (450 g) boneless, skinless chicken breasts, cut into ½-inch (1.25 cm) cubes, chilled

6 ounces (170 g) boneless pork shoulder or other braising cut, diced, chilled

1 large egg, chilled

2 ounces (55 g) shallots, finely chopped

¼ cup (15 g) roughly chopped fresh tarragon or chives

1 teaspoon fine sea salt

½ teaspoon dried thyme

½ teaspoon finely chopped dried rosemary

⅛ teaspoon freshly ground black pepper

⅛ teaspoon freshly grated nutmeg

1 teaspoon bacon fat, duck fat, or unsalted butter

⅓ cup (45 g) raw pistachios

Make the terrine the day before serving. In a bowl, moisten the bread with the milk and Cognac. Refrigerate for 30 minutes.

In a food processor, combine the bread mixture with one-third of the chicken, one-third of the pork, and the egg. Process until finely ground; avoid overprocessing. Transfer to a large bowl. Add the remaining chicken and pork, along with the shallots, tarragon, salt, thyme, rosemary, black pepper, and nutmeg. Stir until thoroughly combined. Scoop out 1 teaspoon of the mixture and cook in a dry skillet over medium heat. Let cool, taste, and adjust the seasoning.

Preheat the oven to 325°F (160°C). Use the bacon fat to grease a 3-cup (720 ml) earthenware terrine about 5 × 7 inches (13 × 18 cm).

Chop 1 tablespoon of the pistachios and set aside for topping.

Layer one-third of the meat into the bottom of the terrine and sprinkle with half the unchopped pistachios. Repeat with another one-third of the meat and the remaining unchopped pistachios. Top with the remaining meat, smooth the surface, and sprinkle on the reserved chopped pistachios. Cover with the lid or a double layer of foil.

Put the terrine in a baking dish large enough to accommodate it and fill the baking dish halfway up with simmering water to create a bain-marie; it allows the terrine to cook evenly. Transfer to the oven and bake 1¼ hours. Remove the lid or foil and bake until golden at the top and thoroughly cooked, 15 minutes longer. A meat thermometer inserted into the center of the terrine should register 160°F (70°C).

Cool completely, cover, and refrigerate 24 hours before serving.

~BEUREKS~
arméniens

ARMENIAN
BYOREKS

MAKES 24 BYOREKS

THE 9TH ARRONDISSEMENT WAS ONCE HOME TO A BUSTLING LITTLE Armenia, first peopled by immigrants who fled the genocide in 1915. The community is more spread out now, but a little node of Armenian spirit remains. The Armenian cultural center operates a restaurant hidden in the back of a paved courtyard at the top of a winding staircase, and the venerable food shop Heratchian Frères, founded in 1925, is a treasure trove of Middle Eastern delicacies. The walls are lined with bulging bags of grains, tall shelves of condiments and spices, buckets of feta cheese, and large trays of hand-folded *byoreks*, bulging triangles of thinly crispy dough filled with ground meat, spinach, pastrami, cheese, and herbs.

I like to make miniature ones to serve with aperitifs. They are easily eaten in two bites, without silverware and without making a mess. Byoreks are fun to assemble, and the preparation can be broken down into steps: Make the filling the day before, bake the byoreks a couple of hours in advance, and reheat before serving.

1 tablespoon olive oil,
plus more for greasing

½ medium yellow onion, diced

1 pound (450 g) fresh spinach,
finely chopped, or 10 ounces
(280 g) frozen spinach, thawed,
squeezed, and roughly chopped

2½ ounces (70 g) feta cheese,
diced

1½ ounces (40 g) thinly sliced
pastrami, chopped

Freshly ground black pepper

12 sheets frozen phyllo
dough (about 14 × 18 inches/
35 × 45 cm), thawed

4 tablespoons (55 g)
unsalted butter, melted

Egg wash: 1 large egg yolk lightly
beaten with 1 teaspoon water

· **NOTES** ·

Traditional byoreks are made with
a special dough called *yufka*, but
store-bought phyllo dough works
just fine.

The byoreks can be baked a few
hours ahead. Reheat for 2 minutes
in a 400°F (200°C) oven.

In a large skillet, heat the olive oil over medium heat. Add the onion and
cook, stirring often, until softened, 2 to 3 minutes. Add the fresh spinach
and cook until just wilted, about 2 minutes (no need to cook the spinach
if using frozen). Drain in a colander for 15 minutes.

Divide the spinach between 2 bowls. Stir the feta into one bowl and the
pastrami in the other. Sprinkle both with pepper. Taste and adjust the
seasoning. (The fillings can be made a day ahead. Cover and refrigerate.)

Preheat the oven to 400°F (200°C). Grease a rimmed baking sheet
with oil.

Stack the 12 sheets of phyllo dough and fold the stack in half like a
book. Cut along the fold to get 24 half-sheets each about 14 × 9 inches
(35 × 23 cm) each. Keep covered with a lightly damp kitchen towel to
prevent drying.

Working on a large cutting board, place 1 sheet phyllo dough with a
short end facing you and brush lightly with butter. Fold in three from the
sides to get a tall and narrow rectangle, about 14 × 3 inches (35 × 7 cm).
Brush with butter again.

Put 1 rounded tablespoon of either of the fillings at the bottom of the
rectangle and fold the bottom right corner over the filling. Fold this triangle
snugly up, then right, then up, then left (like folding a flag), working your way
up to the top of the rectangle. Put seam side down on the prepared baking
sheet. Repeat with the rest of the phyllo sheets and fillings.

Brush the tops with the egg wash and bake until golden brown, about
12 minutes. Cool 10 to 15 minutes before serving.

RADISH LEAF
PESTO

SPRINGTIME MARKET STALLS BOAST BUNCHES OF PINK AND WHITE radishes, sweet and piquant, stacked high, their thin wispy roots making them look like the backsides of so many cartoon mice. The French mostly eat them raw at *apéritif* time, with salted butter and bread, or an herbed yogurt sauce.

But the leaves are edible, too. As soon as a bunch crosses my threshold, my first order of business is to trim the leaves, sorting out the vibrant ones from the yellowing, and washing well to remove the sand. Radish leaves can be cooked like any green and make a fine soup with a potato and some chicken stock; or they can be eaten raw as in this pesto-style spread that honors the Parisian tradition of herb sauces. I spread it on thin slices of baguette to serve with a predinner drink, or toss it with fusilli for dinner.

2 cups (70 g) radish leaves, trimmed

1 ounce (30 g) hard cheese, such as Comté or Parmesan, freshly grated

⅓ cup (50 g) pine nuts, almonds, or pistachios

1 garlic clove, chopped

⅓ cup (80 ml) olive oil, plus more as needed

½ teaspoon fine sea salt

Freshly ground black pepper

In a food processor or blender, combine the radish leaves, cheese, pine nuts, garlic, olive oil, salt, and pepper to taste and process in short pulses until smooth, scraping down the sides. Add a little more oil as needed and pulse again to get the consistency you prefer: thicker for a spread, thinner for a pasta sauce.

Taste, adjust the seasoning, and pack into an airtight glass container. Use within 3 to 4 days. The surface will darken from oxidation, but this won't affect the taste. Top with a thin layer of oil before storing if it bothers you.

BUTTERNUT KIBBEH WITH SPINACH

SERVES 6

IF WE HAVE FRIENDS OVER FOR A PREDINNER DRINK AND I WANT TO SET out a more substantial spread that may in fact replace dinner, this is called an *apéro dînatoire*. A favorite option in the fall and winter is the butternut squash kibbeh, a delectable Lebanese croquette made with a well-seasoned squash purée and bulgur. The pointy dumplings are stuffed with a surprise lump of cooked spinach, baked until crispy, and served with tahini sauce. They are delightful, and a wonderful change of pace when winter squash fatigue sets in.

Kibbeh are also good in a pita pocket with crudités for lunch. Or for a quicker preparation, you can bake this into a big casserole to serve as a main course with a green salad (see Variation).

· NOTE ·

Fine-grind bulgur is available from Middle Eastern markets. Large-grind bulgur can be ground to a finer consistency in a food processor or sturdy blender.

2 pounds (1 kg) butternut squash or other firm-flesh winter squash, cut into 1-inch (2.5 cm) cubes

2 teaspoons fine sea salt

1 cup (200 g) fine-grind bulgur (see Note)

¼ cup (30 g) all-purpose flour

1 teaspoon ground cumin

1 teaspoon ground cinnamon

1 tablespoon freshly squeezed lemon juice

2 tablespoons olive oil, plus more for greasing

1 small yellow onion, thinly sliced

1 pound (450 g) spinach, thinly sliced, or 10 ounces (280 g) frozen spinach, thawed, squeezed, and roughly chopped

½ cup (50 g) walnuts, chopped

FOR THE TAHINI SAUCE

¼ cup (60 ml) tahini

2 tablespoons freshly squeezed lemon juice

1 teaspoon fine sea salt

Put the squash in a large saucepan, add 1 teaspoon of the salt, cover with water, and bring to a simmer. Simmer until soft, about 15 minutes. Drain in a colander for 15 minutes.

Transfer to a large bowl and mash finely with a potato masher or fork. Add the bulgur, flour, cumin, cinnamon, lemon juice, 1 tablespoon of the olive oil, and ½ teaspoon of the salt. Cover and let rest for 1 hour. (This can be prepared up to a day ahead; store refrigerated.)

In a large skillet, heat the remaining 1 tablespoon olive oil over medium heat. Add the onion and cook, stirring frequently, until softened, about 3 minutes. Add the spinach and remaining ½ teaspoon salt and cook until just wilted. Transfer to a colander and drain for 15 minutes. Stir in the walnuts. (This can be prepared a day ahead; cover and refrigerate.)

Preheat the oven to 400°F (200°C). Grease a baking sheet with olive oil.

Bake as a casserole in a medium baking dish, such as a square 8-inch (20 cm) ceramic or glass dish. Spread half the squash mixture onto the bottom, arrange the spinach filling on top, and cover with the remaining squash. Draw a crisscross pattern on the top with the tines of a fork and bake in a 400°F (200°C) oven until set and lightly browned, 30 to 40 minutes. Serve with a green salad.

Scoop ¼ cup (60 ml) of the squash mixture and flatten into an oval on your palm. Put a rounded tablespoon of spinach filling in the center and close the squash over it, forming it into a football shape. Put on the baking sheet and repeat with the remaining ingredients. Bake until set and lightly browned, 30 to 35 minutes.

While the kibbeh are baking, make the tahini sauce: In a bowl, stir together the tahini, lemon juice, and salt with a fork. Thin with 3 to 4 tablespoons water, adding it slowly to prevent curdling. Taste and adjust the seasoning.

Cool the kibbeh for 5 minutes and serve with the sauce alongside for dipping.

PASCADE IS A THICK SAVORY CRÊPE FROM AVEYRON, IN THE CENTER OF France, traditionally made at Easter (*Pâques* in French), which is what the name derives from. The recipe was originally meant to use up the eggs that had piled up, uneaten, during Lent. If ever a dish was more than the sum of its parts, this is it. The simple batter cooks up to an astonishing texture, halfway between a crêpe and a soufflé, crisp on the outside and comfortingly tender inside. Think of it as the French cousin to the Dutch baby pancake.

Pascade is the focus of a same-name Parisian restaurant created by Michelin-starred chef Alexandre Bourdas. He uses the dish to compose edible tableaux of seasonal ingredients: lightly dressed greens, shavings of cheese, and pickled onions on top; thin slices of radishes and turnips with an herb coulis; mâche leaves with sticks of green apple and thinly sliced prosciutto.

Pascade is a natural fit for brunch, but I like it even better in early evening, served with sparkling white wine. I cut the pascade in thin wedges, shower with snipped chives, and serve in the pan for guests to grab and eat.

~PASCADE~

OVEN-PUFFED PANCAKE

SERVES 4

3 large eggs

1 cup (130 g) all-purpose flour

¼ teaspoon fine sea salt

1¼ cups (300 ml) whole milk

3 tablespoons (40 g) unsalted butter

Finely chopped fresh chives

Preheat the oven to 425°F (220°C).

In a medium bowl, whisk together the eggs, flour, and salt. Whisk the milk in slowly, until the batter is smooth. (Alternatively, combine all the ingredients in a blender and blend on medium-high for a few seconds.)

Put the butter in a 10-inch (25 cm) ovenproof cast-iron pan and put in the oven until just melted, watching carefully so it doesn't burn. As soon as the butter is melted, remove the pan and swirl to spread the butter. Pour the batter in gently, then return to the oven and bake until puffy and golden brown, 20 to 25 minutes. (It will collapse when it comes out.)

Using kitchen scissors, cut the pancake into thin wedges. Sprinkle with chives and serve.

· **VARIATIONS** ·
You can fold finely chopped herbs and/or grated cheese into the batter.

WINE BARS, WINE SHOPS & NATURAL WINES

WINE IS FRANCE'S MOST ICONIC AND BELOVED ALCOHOLIC BEVERAGE, far ahead of beer or any hard liquor. It is an integral part of the French meal experience, and depending on how well stocked their wine cellar is, restaurants present their guests with a one-page selection or a phone book of a list. But Parisians love to relax in *bars à vin*, casual wine bars with a chummy atmosphere and a few simple nibbles. They love to drink wine at home as well, buying it from one of the many independent *cavistes* (wine shops) focusing on natural wines that have sprouted up in recent years.

The natural wine movement was started by artisan vintners in reaction to the chemically manipulated, mass-produced wines flooding the market in France and abroad. Their ambition is to go back to the essence of wine as fermented grape juice—nothing more, nothing less—letting the grapes and the soil speak for themselves, intervening as little as possible in their natural expression.

France does not regulate the terms *vin naturel, vin nature,* or *vin en biodynamie,* so the only way to know what you're drinking, short of inspecting vineyards, is to place your trust in cavistes or restaurant owners who have established a relationship with the vintners they distribute, and have also thoroughly acquainted themselves with the vintners' winemaking approach.

Tchin tchin ! (That's "cheers" in French.)

~MOULES GRATINÉES~
à l'ail et au persil

GRATINÉED MUSSELS
WITH GARLIC & PARSLEY

SERVES 4 TO 6

FRENCH MUSSELS ARE TRADITIONALLY SOLD BY VOLUME IN FRANCE: Tell the fishmonger how many liters you want—one liter is about 1½ pounds—and they'll use a dedicated bucket to scoop that amount from the big pile of glistening black shells.

I adore mussels and their briny, nutty chew, but I find them bothersome to clean in large amounts, so I use them in recipes where a little goes a long way, such as these gratinéed ones I offer as a finger food, with glasses of dry white wine.

1½ pounds (700 g) mussels (about 30 large)

3 tablespoons (45 g) unsalted butter, at room temperature

2 ounces (55 g) shallots, finely chopped

1 teaspoon fine sea salt

1 cup (240 ml) dry white wine or fish stock

3 tablespoons unseasoned bread crumbs (see Making Your Own Bread Crumbs, page 18)

¼ cup (15 g) finely chopped fresh flat-leaf parsley

1 garlic clove, finely chopped

½ lemon, for serving

Crusty bread, for serving

Cover the mussels with fresh water in the sink and shuffle to scrub. Set a large colander over a large bowl. Examine each mussel. If the shell is broken or chipped, discard. If the shell is ajar, tap with your fingernail; if the mussel doesn't slowly close, discard it. Mussels have a tuft of dark stringy hairs; pull it gently but firmly and discard. Put the mussels in the colander. Return to the sink and rinse in two to three more baths of fresh water. Drain.

In a heavy pot, melt 1 teaspoon of the butter over medium-high heat. Add the shallots and ½ teaspoon of the salt and cook, stirring often, until softened, about 3 minutes. Add the mussels and wine and cook, stirring regularly, until the mussels open, 4 to 5 minutes. Discard any that don't by this time.

Lift the mussels with tongs or a slotted spoon. (Reserve the broth to drink or use for fish stew. The mussels can be cooked up to 8 hours ahead. Cool, cover, and refrigerate.)

In a bowl, mash together the remaining butter, bread crumbs, parsley, garlic, and remaining ½ teaspoon salt. (This can be prepared up to a day ahead. Cover and refrigerate; soften before using.)

Preheat the broiler. Tear off the top shell from each mussel and loosen the meat from the bottom shell. Put the bottom shells with the mussel meat on a rimmed baking sheet. Divide the butter topping among the mussels. Broil until golden and bubbling, about 2 minutes.

Transfer to a serving platter. Squeeze lemon juice over the mussels and serve with toothpicks and crusty bread.

IT IS DIFFICULT AND EXPENSIVE TO OBTAIN THE LICENCE IV ("LICENSE 4")
that allows French bars to sell alcoholic beverages on their own (with no
food); it is much easier to get a restaurant-type liquor license, authorizing
the sale of alcohol only in the context of a meal. In Paris, this has led to
the creation of many little wine bars that offer small plates and nibbles
with the wine they serve.

I love what they create, often with minimal space and equipment, as well
as the casual flexibility of these bars: Get there in early evening to catch up
with a friend over a drink and marinated olives, and if the conversation is
as good as the wine, it may extend into the night as you order more small
plates, graduating to more filling ones.

One such dish is the *camembert au four*, a baked Camembert cheese that
is brought to the table, bubbling and fragrant, like a miniature fondue. In
keeping with the origins of a genuine Camembert, I flavor mine with apple
cider or brandy from Normandy, and a touch of honey.

~CAMEMBERT~
au four, miel et cidre

BAKED CAMEMBERT
WITH HONEY
&
APPLE CIDER

SERVES 4

8 to 9 ounces (220 to 250 g)
Camembert cheese (see Note)

1 tablespoon hard apple cider
or apple brandy, such as Calvados

2 teaspoons honey

Fresh baguette, for serving

Remove the cheese from the refrigerator 1 hour before you begin. Strip
it of its box and wrapper, remove any sticker or label, and put it in an
ovenproof bowl or baking dish in which it fits snugly but not too tightly.

Preheat the oven to 400°F (200°C).

Using a sharp knife, make deep cuts across the top of the Camembert in
a crosshatch pattern. Drizzle with the apple cider and spoon the honey
on top. Bake until melted and browning, 15 to 20 minutes. Let stand for
5 minutes before serving with bread.

· NOTE ·

The authentic Camembert cheese
is the Camembert de Normandie,
protected by an appellation
of origin. It is made with raw
milk, so it can't be imported
into North America, but other
French Camemberts made with
pasteurized milk are; I recommend
you seek those out.

FRENCH APÉRITIFS

AN *APÉRITIF* BEFORE DINNER IS MEANT TO STIMULATE THE APPETITE, WHICH is what the word means. Some beverages are considered more appropriate to that task: White wine (still or sparkling), a light red, and rosé in summer are straightforward choices, and craft cocktails are increasingly popular.

For a fun change of pace, I order old-school French apéritifs such as Lillet (white, rosé, or red), which is a blend of Bordeaux wine and citrus liqueurs, or Suze, a bittersweet apéritif distilled from gentian root. Kir, a mix of white Burgundy and crème de cassis (blackcurrant liqueur), is considered a little passé—so perhaps it's due for a comeback.

MY DEAR AMERICAN FRIEND EMILY IS MARRIED TO A FRENCHMAN NAMED (of course) Bruno, and they have the good fortune of living in an apartment with a full view of the Eiffel Tower. Every summer, on Bastille Day, they invite those of their friends still in the city for a special *apéritif* and a viewing of the gorgeous fireworks, the adults mesmerized and the children squealing.

The edible spread is assembled potluck-style, and guests are tasked with bringing something "very French." I whip out my beloved recipe for *cake salé*, a quick bread and a staple of French apéritifs and picnics. Mine is crusty and moist, and I present it in slices or cubes.

This olive and goat cheese filling is a classic, but the basic batter welcomes any combo. Stick to two to three flavors max: feta cheese and fresh herbs; Gruyère and ham; mushrooms and bacon; pears, walnuts, and blue cheese; tuna and dill.

Unsalted butter, for greasing

3 tablespoons white sesame seeds

1¼ cups (150 g) all-purpose flour

1 tablespoon baking powder

3 large eggs

¼ cup (60 ml) olive oil

½ cup plus 2 tablespoons (150 g) plain whole-milk yogurt

1 tablespoon mixed dried herbs, such as herbes de Provence, or 1 tablespoon pesto

¼ teaspoon fine sea salt

¼ teaspoon freshly ground black pepper

3½ ounces (100 g) pitted green olives

3½ ounces (100 g) pitted black olives

5 ounces (140 g) fresh goat cheese, such as a log, cut into ½-inch (1.25 cm) cubes

· NOTE ·

The bread can be frozen, tightly wrapped. Thaw overnight in the fridge.

Preheat the oven to 350°F (175°C). Grease a 9 × 5-inch (24 × 12 cm) loaf pan with butter and sprinkle half the sesame seeds evenly onto the bottom and sides.

In a bowl, combine the flour and baking powder in a bowl. In a separate medium bowl, whisk together the eggs, oil, yogurt, herbs, salt, and pepper. Stir in the olives and goat cheese. Fold the flour mixture into the egg mixture. Don't overmix; it's okay if a few lumps remain.

Pour into the loaf pan, smooth with a spatula, and sprinkle with the remaining sesame seeds. Bake until the loaf is golden and a cake tester inserted into the center comes out clean, 40 to 50 minutes.

Let cool for 5 to 10 minutes in the pan, then run a knife around the pan to loosen. Unmold and transfer to a rack to cool. Cut into slices or cubes just before serving, slightly warm or at room temperature.

~GUÊPE VERTE~

GREEN WASP

COCKTAIL

SERVES 1 (CAN BE DOUBLED)

GO TO CANDELARIA, ON A SMALL STREET OF THE UPPER MARAIS, AND AT first you'll think I've sent you to a tiny taqueria. I have, and if you need your taco fix in Paris, these won't disappoint. But what I want you to do is head to the back, push the unmarked door, and walk into the hidden craft cocktail bar behind it, roomy and romantic with wood and copper accents, dim lighting, and stone walls. This is a major site in the renaissance of cocktails that started in Paris in the second half of the naughts.

La Guêpe Verte ("the green wasp") is the signature cocktail at Candelaria: a refreshing, spicy short drink mixed from tequila, lime, cilantro, and cucumber—a bit like a mojito, only zestier and with a better story.

3 to 4 large ice cubes

4 slices cucumber
(about ¼ inch/6 mm thick)

3 tablespoons fresh
cilantro leaves

4 teaspoons (20 ml)
freshly squeezed lime juice

4 teaspoons (20 ml) agave syrup

3½ tablespoons (50 ml) chile-infused 100% agave tequila blanco or plata (store-bought or homemade; see Chile-Infused Tequila, left)

Put a cocktail shaker and lowball glass in the refrigerator 1 hour before serving.

When ready to mix the cocktail, put the ice cubes in the glass so they reach slightly higher than the rim. Put 3 cucumber slices and the cilantro in the shaker and, using a long muddler, press once and twist a few times, until the smell of cucumber and cilantro rises. Add the lime juice, agave syrup, and tequila. Fill the shaker with ice and shake until well chilled, 15 to 20 seconds. Strain into the glass. Garnish with the remaining cucumber slice and serve with 2 short straws.

 **CHILE-INFUSED TEQUILA**
You can buy spicy tequila from well-stocked liquor stores, or make it yourself. Pour 1¼ cups (300 ml) 100% agave tequila blanco (also labeled plata or silver) in a glass jar with a lid. Add 3 small red chiles, fresh or dried, halved lengthwise (remove the seeds for less heat), and infuse for 24 hours, shaking once or twice. Strain and return to the jar; this is enough for 6 Guêpes Vertes.

LOOKING FOR A SIMPLE BUT FESTIVE COCKTAIL TO CELEBRATE A BIRTHDAY or holiday? The French 75 is your guy. A subtle mix of gin and Champagne with fresh lemon juice and a touch of sugar, it is named after a quick-firing artillery gun the French used during World War I. It is said to have been created in the aftermath of the war by Harry MacElhone, the bartender at Harry's New York Bar near the Paris Opera. Over the decades, this legendary bar has served as a haven for American artists and international celebrities.

Sour and punchy, the *soixante-quinze* is my cocktail when I go out. And if you ever find yourself with leftover bubbly—it happens to some people— it is the perfect cocktail to use it in the next day.

~SOIXANTE-QUINZE~

FRENCH 75

SERVES 1
(CAN BE DOUBLED)

1½ ounces (45 ml) London dry gin or Cognac

½ ounce (15 ml) freshly squeezed lemon juice

1 teaspoon superfine sugar

2 to 3 ounces (60 to 90 ml) brut Champagne or other sparkling dry white wine, chilled

1 long thin strip of lemon zest

· **NOTE** ·
If hosting a crowd, mix a big batch of the gin, lemon juice, and sugar ahead of time, scaling the recipe as needed, and keep chilled. To serve, pour 2 ounces (¼ cup/60 ml) in each glass and top up with Champagne.

Put a cocktail shaker and a Champagne flute in the refrigerator 1 hour before serving.

When ready to mix the cocktail, fill the shaker with ice. Add the gin, lemon juice, and sugar and shake until well chilled, 15 to 20 seconds. Strain into the flute. Top with Champagne. Wrap the zest around your finger to create a curl, lower into the glass, and serve.

CHEESE & CHARCUTERIE BOARDS

WHEN GATHERING WITH FRIENDS AT A WINE BAR, IF YOU THINK YOU might make a meal out of it, it is popular to order with your drink a cheese and/or charcuterie board: *une planche de fromage, de charcuterie,* or *une planche mixte,* with both.

This comes on a wooden cutting board featuring assorted pieces of cheese (different milk types and aging styles) or pork products (thinly sliced dry sausage and country ham, a pâté or terrine of some kind), with some cornichons (never enough of them; I ask for more) and a basket of fresh bread. Depending on the gastronomic aspirations of the owners, the quality of the selection will vary, but the average level is high and the most modest wine bar can be trusted to provide a satisfying one.

It's also an easy item to re-create at home; a joyful and low-effort offering when hosting friends in early evening.

SIDECAR

SERVES 1

ONE OF THE MOST FAMOUS BARS IN THE WORLD, BAR HEMINGWAY HIDES in the depths of the Ritz Hotel, and Colin Peter Field, its head bartender since 1994, has received multiple international awards. He serves an extravagant version of the Sidecar, invented at the Ritz in 1923: It uses a specific brand of Cognac predating the phylloxera epidemic that devastated French vineyards in the 1880s. Unsurprisingly, it is one of the most expensive drinks you will ever see listed on a bar menu.

Regardless of the brandy you use, this is a great cocktail to have up your sleeve, and not just because you can't not smile when thinking of an actual sidecar (right?). I follow the easy formula sanctioned by Orr Shtuhl, who authored the witty *Illustrated Guide to Cocktails*: a 3½-2-1 mix of Cognac, Cointreau, and lemon juice—the same ratio of liquor to triple sec to citrus juice as in a margarita, or Kamikaze, or Cosmopolitan. Commit this to memory and you'll make friends everywhere you go.

1¼ ounces (35 ml) Cognac

4 teaspoons (20 ml) Cointreau

2 teaspoons (10 ml) freshly squeezed lemon juice

1 thin strip of orange zest

Put a cocktail shaker and a martini glass in the refrigerator 1 hour before serving.

When ready to mix the cocktail, fill the shaker with ice. Add the Cognac, Cointreau, and lemon juice and shake until well chilled, 15 to 20 seconds. Strain into the glass, add the orange zest, and serve.

EVENING

LE SOIR

À Paris y a pas d'parking
Mais qu'elle est belle
La Tour Eiffel
—**RIFF COHEN**

NOT A WEEK GOES BY THAT MY LIST OF "EXCITING RESTAURANTS I simply must try" (actual name of my spreadsheet) doesn't grow longer by several new names. I can't keep up, and I remain energized by the city's vibrant activity.

In Paris, the unique combination of reasonably priced leases and an international reputation for gastronomic excellence has created fertile ground for culinary creativity. Well-traveled young chefs from France and abroad settle here, and pack the tiniest spaces with their bold personalities and flavors.

For special occasions, I am also drawn to more upscale establishments, where every dish is a little tableau, attention to detail is everywhere, and service and hospitality are elevated to an art form. These meals feel like they're out of time, a bubble of bliss best shared with someone you love.

From these diverse dining experiences, Parisians emerge well fed and inspired, and often take dish ideas into their own kitchens for when they have guests over, which they love to do despite living in small spaces. It is not about pretending they're a professional chef if they're not, but rather taking a clever idea—a pairing, a cooking method, a plating trick—and running with it, making it their own and serving it with that uniquely French, one-shoulder shrug that says both "I've put a lot of thought into this for you" and "I hardly broke a sweat."

These recipes are the kind that make an impression without requiring tremendous work, and teach you valuable techniques along the way.

~COEURS DE ROMAINE~
aux poires et au bleu

ROMAINE HEARTS
WITH PEARS
&
BLUE CHEESE

SERVES 4

is the fairly low barrier to entry: It is still possible for young French chefs to find affordable spaces, without getting investors on board, which goes a long way to preserving their creative spontaneity.

I am fond of Comptoir Canailles, a small bistro run by a couple in their late twenties who serve inspired, market-driven dishes. Theirs is the kind of simple yet expertly crafted food that leaves me scribbling furiously in my notebook to remember some idea, some pairing I can take away for my own cooking.

This is the very first starter I ever ate there: A couple of wedges of crisp lettuce receive a drizzle of creamy blue cheese dressing—the chef uses Bleu d'Auvergne—and a scattering of crumbled walnuts and pear slivers. It is a quintessentially French salad, bold and unmistakable.

3 tablespoons (45 ml) heavy cream

3½ ounces (100 g) blue cheese, such as Roquefort or Bleu d'Auvergne

¼ cup (60 ml) Bistro Vinaigrette (page 54)

1 large head romaine lettuce (10 ounces/280 g), outer leaves removed, sliced lengthwise into 8 wedges, keeping the core to hold the wedges in shape

Freshly ground black pepper

1 medium pear, cored and cut into thin vertical slices

½ cup (50 g) walnuts, lightly toasted

Crusty bread, for serving

Start the dressing 2 hours in advance or up to 1 day before serving.

In a small saucepan, combine the cream and half the cheese. Bring to a simmer over low heat, whisking to dissolve the cheese. Transfer to a bowl, cover, and refrigerate. Remove 1 hour before serving.

When ready to eat, whisk the vinaigrette into the bowl of creamed blue cheese. It will be thick.

Put 2 wedges of lettuce on each plate. Spoon the blue cheese dressing on top, and sprinkle with black pepper. Crumble the remaining blue cheese over the lettuce hearts. Arrange the pear slices on and around the lettuce and sprinkle with the walnuts. Serve with crusty bread.

~SOUPE~
de courge rôtie, quenelle
de fromage frais au curry

ROASTED SQUASH SOUP

&

CURRIED CHEESE QUENELLE

SERVES 4

· **NOTE** ·

If you're using an early fall organic squash with thin skin, it's not necessary to peel it.

IN FRANCE, YOUNG PROFESSIONALS TRAIN IN *ÉCOLES HÔTELIÈRES*, schools that teach them the exacting rules that govern proper restaurant service. Tableside service—when a member of the waitstaff finishes a dish in front of you with precise choreographed gestures—is especially valued.

Soups can receive this special treatment: The waiter first brings a soup plate that contains, intriguingly, a simple scatter of tiny vegetables or a quenelle (oval scoop) of something creamy. Seconds later he returns with a spouted pot and pours the soup into the plate, so you can enjoy the sight and smell of it, and witness the moment when the velvety liquid engulfs the garnishes.

For this roasted squash soup, which I make often in the fall and winter, I whip up a quick bowl of curried goat cheese and scoop it into the bowls before serving the soup—an easy but sophisticated touch.

3 tablespoons olive oil, plus more for the baking sheet

2 pounds (900 g) firm-flesh winter squash, such as butternut, delicata, or red kuri, peeled (see Note) and cut into 2-inch (5 cm) wedges or slices

Fine sea salt

Up to 4 cups (1 liter) vegetable or chicken stock, warmed

5¼ ounces (150 g) fresh goat cheese

2 teaspoons freshly squeezed lemon juice

¼ cup (15 g) finely chopped fresh flat-leaf parsley

½ teaspoon curry powder

Quick Croutons (page 62)

Freshly ground black pepper

Preheat the oven to 400°F (200°C). Grease a rimmed baking sheet with olive oil.

Put the squash on the baking sheet and drizzle with 2 tablespoons of the olive oil and ½ teaspoon salt. Roast until cooked through and very tender, 30 to 40 minutes.

In a blender, combine the squash with 3 cups (720 ml) of the stock and process until smooth and pourable, adding more stock as needed. Taste and adjust the seasoning. (This can be prepared up to a day ahead. Cover, refrigerate, and reheat before serving.)

In a bowl using a fork, mash the goat cheese with the remaining 1 tablespoon olive oil and the lemon juice, parsley, and curry powder. (This can be prepared up to a day ahead. Cover and refrigerate.)

Transfer the hot soup to a pitcher with a pouring spout.

Using two tablespoons, shape the cheese into 4 quenelles and put one in the center of each of 4 bowls or soup plates. Scatter a few croutons around it and sprinkle with black pepper. Bring the bowls to the table and pour soup over each without disturbing the quenelle. Serve with more croutons.

PARIS HAS NOT ONE, NOT TWO, BUT THREE DIFFERENT CHINATOWNS.
The longest established is in the Marais, around rue Volta. Next up is
Belleville, where Asian immigrants gained ground over the local North
African community. Finally, there's the Quartier Chinois in the 13th
arrondissement, in the southeast corner of the city, the largest Chinatown
in Europe, founded in the seventies by refugees from Vietnam, Laos, and
Cambodia. A large Chinese population joined their ranks, and together
they run the majority of businesses in the area.

It is not the most picturesque of Chinatowns, with its high-rise apartment
buildings and aging shopping center, but the wide sidewalks and village
atmosphere make it lovely for a stroll and a bite. When I'm feeling under
the weather, I'll get the ingredients to make this rice and ginger soup, a
traditional flu remedy for children in Chinese and Vietnamese families;
I save the back of the chicken I cut up for Lemon Spatchcocked Chicken
(page 197) just for this.

½ cup (90 g) long-grain white rice

¼ cup (45 g) sticky rice

1 tablespoon neutral oil, such as
sunflower seed, grapeseed,
or canola

1-inch (2.5 cm) piece fresh ginger,
peeled and finely minced

2 garlic cloves, finely minced

2 scallions (white and green
parts), thinly sliced

Fine sea salt

1 cup (25 g) dried mushroom slices,
preferably shiitake

6 to 12 ounces (170 to 340 g)
chicken (thigh, leg, breast,
or back)

¼ cup (60 ml) fish sauce

Roughly chopped fresh cilantro,
for serving

Thinly sliced fresh red chiles,
for serving (optional)

1 lime, cut into wedges, for serving

· **VARIATION** ·
You can make this with pork or
beef, sliced or ground; reduce the
meat cooking time to 20 minutes.

Rinse the rices in a fine-mesh sieve for just a few seconds to remove
impurities. (Don't wash away the starch.)

In a heavy-bottomed pot, heat the oil over medium heat. Add the ginger,
garlic, scallions, and ¾ teaspoon salt. Cook until lightly colored, about
2 minutes. Add the rice and cook until lightly toasted, another 4 minutes.
Add the mushrooms, chicken, and 4 cups (960 ml) water. Simmer until
the rice is cooked through, about 20 minutes. Add 4 more cups (960 ml)
water and cook until the chicken falls off the bones, 40 minutes more.

Remove the chicken from the pot and pull the meat off the bone (discard
the bones and skin). Shred the meat roughly with a fork and return to the
pot. Stir in the fish sauce and add a little more water as needed to create
a brothy soup. Taste and adjust the seasoning.

Ladle into bowls and top with cilantro and sliced chile peppers, if
desired. Serve with lime wedges for squeezing.

~CHOU-FLEUR~
en brioche

CAULIFLOWER
BRIOCHE

SERVES 8
AS A FIRST COURSE

· **NOTES** ·

At the Plaza Athénée, the cauliflower wedge is generously sprinkled with shavings of white truffle. If you have a truffle lying around, you know what to do.

The roasted cauliflower sauce on its own makes a wondrous soup. Thin it with an extra cup of water or stock, and serve with Quick Croutons (page 62) and snipped herbs.

WHEN LUXURY PARIS HOTEL THE PLAZA ATHÉNÉE REOPENED AFTER A renovation, there was much talk about its gastronomic restaurant going pescatarian. Say what? No meat at all? Not even a little chicken? No. The menu focused on seasonal vegetables, organic grains, and sustainably sourced seafood, all under the watchful eye of Alain Ducasse, the French resto-preneur, with executive chef Romain Meder, both seeking to start a discussion about sourcing and sustainability in this conservative sphere.

Among the most memorable dishes I ate there was the *chou-fleur en fine croûte*, a head of cauliflower baked in brioche dough. The waiter brought it to us whole on a wheeled side table and sliced the shiny globe with reverence, transferring wedges onto our plates. The buttery brioche, the nutty cauliflower, the happy surprise of Comté cheese oozing from between the florets—all came together into a glorious vegetarian dish that will easily take center stage for a special dinner or holiday meal.

Please don't be intimidated by this four-part recipe; it is not difficult and many of the steps can be done the day before.

Morning Brioche (page 26)

FOR THE SAUCE

1¼ pounds (600 g) cauliflower (about ½ head), cut into 1-inch (2.5 cm) florets

1 medium yellow onion, minced

2 tablespoons olive oil

½ teaspoon fine sea salt

5 ounces (140 g) Comté cheese, cubed

2 cups (480 ml) chicken or vegetable stock

FOR THE CAULIFLOWER

1 large head (about 2½ pounds/ 1.2 kg) cauliflower, leaves and ribs removed, bottom trimmed to sit flat

3½ ounces (100 g) Comté cheese, cut into 1-inch (2.5 cm) sticks

Egg wash: 1 large egg, lightly beaten with a pinch of salt and 2 teaspoons water

Fleur de sel

Freshly ground black pepper

Fresh chervil or tarragon, for serving

The day before serving, prepare the brioche dough through the step instructing you to put the dough in the fridge overnight.

MAKE THE SAUCE UP TO A DAY BEFORE SERVING: Preheat the oven to 400°F (200°C).

Put the cauliflower florets and onion on a rimmed baking sheet. Add the olive oil and salt and toss to coat. Roast until the cauliflower is caramelized at the edges, 20 to 25 minutes. Add the Comté and bake until the cheese turns golden, another 5 to 10 minutes. Transfer to a

(recipe continues)

blender, including all the caramelized bits. Add the stock and process until smooth. (If making a day ahead, let cool, cover, and refrigerate.)

PREPARE THE CAULIFLOWER: In a steamer, cook the whole head of cauliflower until cooked through but still al dente, about 20 minutes. Cool completely. (You can make this the day before. Let cool, cover, and refrigerate.)

When ready to cook, line a baking sheet with parchment paper.

Insert sticks of Comté between and into the florets of the cooled cauliflower head.

Remove the brioche dough from the refrigerator. Divide in half. (You only need half the brioche dough here. The extra half can be frozen; see Notes on page 26.)

On a lightly floured surface, roll the dough into a round just large enough to wrap around the cauliflower head. Brush off the excess flour. Put the cauliflower head upside down in the middle of the round and fold the dough up and over the cauliflower. Put the wrapped cauliflower seam side down on the baking sheet. Brush the top and sides with some of the egg wash (refrigerate the remaining egg wash) and let rest at room temperature for 1 hour.

Preheat the oven to 350°F (175°C).

Brush the brioche again with the remaining egg wash and bake until golden brown and puffy, 20 to 25 minutes.

Reheat the cauliflower sauce.

Bring the brioche to the table and cut into wedges with a serrated knife. Spoon some sauce on each plate, top with a cauliflower slice, and sprinkle with fleur de sel, black pepper, and snipped chervil before serving.

BISTRO, BRASSERIE, RESTAURANT, CAFÉ

PARIS RESTAURANTS HAVE UNDERGONE MANY TRANSFORMATIONS SINCE their birth in the eighteenth century (see page 10), as different styles have sprouted up and branched out over the decades.

Le restaurant is the umbrella term used for any business where meals are served in exchange for payment, from the simplest neighborhood place to the most upscale gastronomic restaurant.

Un bistro (or *bistrot*) is a small and unpretentious restaurant, independently owned, with a short menu of market dishes. The average bistro has modest gastronomic ambitions; gastro-bistros are more chef-focused and have higher standards.

Une brasserie was originally a restaurant that served beer—*brasserie* means "brewery"—and hearty fare, often of Alsatian inspiration. The word is now used more broadly for traditional restaurants, larger and less personal than bistros, that offer a longer menu of set classics served nonstop throughout the day.

Un café is primarily a place to get drinks, seated at a table or standing at the bar. Most cafés have croissants available in the morning, and a menu of lunchtime basics: big salads, quiches, croque-madame, a *plat du jour* . . .

I WASN'T YET BORN WHEN THE CENTRAL FOOD MARKET WAS TAKEN OUT of the heart of Paris in the mid-seventies, the glass-and-iron pavilions of Les Halles torn down, and the new wholesale food market—now the largest in Europe—relocated outside the city, in Rungis. But I did grow up with the vivid descriptions in Zola's *The Belly of Paris*, the colorful tales told by my own grandmother, and the unglamorous mall built in the old market's place. But now the neighborhood is turning over a new leaf, introducing a freshly landscaped garden and gleaming new restaurants.

At the forefront of them is Champeaux, a contemporary brasserie reviving beloved classics like soufflés and onion soup and croque-monsieur. The kitchen offers an exceptional roast chicken for which the bird is spatchcocked (split open so it cooks flat), marinated in lemon juice and olive oil, and roasted until golden brown and irresistibly fragrant. It is a game-changing technique that produces a finger-licking chicken through minimal effort, and is plenty company-worthy. Serve it with an arugula salad dressed with Bistro Vinaigrette (page 54) and mashed potatoes.

~POULET~
en crapaudine au citron

LEMON SPATCHCOCKED CHICKEN

SERVES 4

· **VARIATION** ·
Add 2 to 3 halved lemons to the dish to roast alongside the chicken.

1 whole chicken (about 3½ pounds/1.6 kg)	½ cup (120 ml) freshly squeezed lemon juice (about 3 lemons)
1 tablespoon fine sea salt	2 tablespoons olive oil

Begin at least 4½ hours before serving. Put the chicken in front of you on a clean cutting board, breast side down, tail end closest to you. Using sturdy kitchen shears, cut the bird along the right side of the backbone, from tail to neck. Turn the chicken around and repeat on the other side of the backbone. (If you're left-handed, reverse.) Save the backbone for chicken stock or Rice and Ginger Soup (page 189).

Flip the chicken breast side up and press firmly down with both palms over the breastbone until the chicken lies flat on the board like a butterfly. (You will hear the bones crack; don't freak out.) Rub the salt on both sides and put the bird in a ceramic or glass baking dish just large enough to accommodate it. Add the lemon juice and olive oil and flip several times to coat, ending up breast side down. Cover with plastic wrap and refrigerate. Marinate for at least 3 hours or overnight, flipping the bird again a couple of times.

Preheat the oven to 425°F (220°C).

Lift the chicken from the baking dish, pour the marinade into a bowl, and return the chicken to the dish. Roast for 45 minutes. Every 10 minutes, baste with 3 tablespoons of the reserved marinade along with the cooking juices. The chicken is done when it is golden brown and a meat thermometer inserted into the fleshy part of the thigh registers 165°F (74°C).

Transfer to a cutting board and carve into 8 serving pieces. Drizzle with the juices from the pan and serve.

TFAYA CHICKEN
COUSCOUS

SERVES 4 TO 6

WHEN THE FRENCH ARE POLLED EVERY YEAR ABOUT THEIR FAVORITE DISHES— yes, it is a thing—couscous always ranks in the top five, a testament to our deep-rooted relationships with Maghreb countries: Morocco, Tunisia, and Algeria were French colonies until the 1950s and '60s.

Setting aside—just for a moment—the history of colonial oppression, cultural exchanges have been rich and numerous through the centuries, and the French gastronomic landscape has benefited. Many North African specialties seem as familiar as French ones in the national psyche, and if you're invited to a Parisian's home, you're more likely to eat a tagine than a blanquette. Part of the appeal is the delicate alliance of sweet and savory, exemplified in this Moroccan couscous. *Tfaya* is a condiment of caramelized onions and raisins that complements a richly flavorful chicken stew, served with couscous, herbs, and roasted almonds.

It is a festive and interactive option for a crowd. The tfaya and chicken can be cooked the day before, so all that is left to do is reheat, cook the couscous, and arrange everything in a large serving dish and side bowls to set on the table.

HOW TO COOK COUSCOUS

Couscous is traditionally prepared in a *couscoussière*, a double pot that stews the meat in the lower part and steams the couscous grains in the upper part. I don't have one, so I cook the couscous separately.

Start 10 minutes before serving. For 4 to 6 servings, measure 1¾ cups (10 ounces or 280 g) uncooked couscous into a large heatproof bowl or serving platter. Add 1 teaspoon fine sea salt and pour in 1¼ cups (300 ml) boiling water. Stir carefully to make sure the grains are evenly moistened. Cover and let rest for 5 minutes for the water to be completely absorbed. Add 2 tablespoons (30 g) butter, diced, and fluff the couscous with a fork as you stir in the butter. Serve immediately.

FOR THE TFAYA

¾ cup (100 g) raisins

2 medium yellow onions, finely minced

1 tablespoon olive oil

1 teaspoon ground cinnamon

¼ teaspoon fine sea salt

1 tablespoon turbinado sugar

1 tablespoon (15 g) unsalted butter

1 tablespoon orange blossom water

FOR THE CHICKEN

1 tablespoon olive oil

1 whole chicken, cut into 8 pieces, or 4 chicken legs, split at the joint (about 3½ pounds/1.5 kg total)

1 medium yellow onion, thinly sliced

2 medium zucchini (about 1 pound/450 g total), halved lengthwise and cut crosswise into 1-inch lengths

¼ cup (60 ml) tomato paste

1 cinnamon stick

1 teaspoon fine sea salt

FOR SERVING

1¾ cups (10 ounces/280 g) couscous, cooked (see How to Cook Couscous, left)

½ cup (70 g) roasted almonds, roughly chopped

½ cup (30 g) roughly chopped fresh flat-leaf parsley

Harissa

(recipe continues)

PREPARE THE TFAYA UP TO A DAY BEFORE SERVING: In a bowl, soak the raisins in boiling water for 10 minutes. Drain.

In a large saucepan, combine the onions, olive oil, ground cinnamon, salt, and ⅔ cup (160 ml) water. Simmer over medium heat until the water is evaporated and the onions are soft, about 5 minutes, stirring regularly. Stir in the raisins, sugar, butter, and orange blossom water and cook, stirring regularly, until caramelized, about 3 minutes. (If making a day ahead, cool, cover, and refrigerate. Reheat before serving.)

COOK THE CHICKEN UP TO A DAY BEFORE SERVING: In a heavy-bottomed pot, heat the olive oil over medium heat. Working in batches if necessary, add the chicken in a single layer and cook until browned on both sides, about 10 minutes, flipping halfway through. When all the chicken is browned, return the pieces to the pot. Stir in the onion, zucchini, tomato paste, cinnamon stick, and salt. Add 2 cups (480 ml) water, cover, and simmer until the chicken is cooked through and very tender, about 1 hour. The flavor will improve overnight. Cool, cover, and refrigerate. Reheat before serving.

TO SERVE: Arrange the cooked couscous in a dome on a wide serving platter. Form a well at the top. Scoop the chicken and vegetables out of the broth with a slotted spoon and place in the center of the couscous. Shower with the roasted almonds and parsley. Serve the tfaya, remaining broth, and harissa in separate bowls for guests to help themselves.

SPICE-CRUSTED
DUCK
MAGRET

SERVES 4

ORDER A MAGRET—THE BREAST OF A FATTENED DUCK—IN A PARISIAN BUTCHER shop and your *garçon-boucher* will score the fat and wrap up the meat like a gift in a parchment package. Then he will look you up and down to gauge your cooking abilities and deliver an off-the-cuff cooking lesson amid the hanging chickens and pig's feet. You'll be given cooking times and temperatures; jot them down or repeat them under your breath on the way home.

The recommended side is always potatoes, regardless of the preparation, and tend toward minimal spices—they want their meat to shine through. I don't tell them that my favorite way to roast duck magret is to rub it with a DIY mix of spices that creates the most delicious crust.

Some of you will see the lavender listed and think "Eww, soapy!" but I promise it will be delicate and balanced, evoking the markets of southern France, not laundry detergent. Serve with Brown Butter Pommes Anna (page 228), just what the butcher ordered.

· **NOTE** ·

If quality, humanely raised duck is difficult to find or expensive, use the rub on chicken or lamb instead.

2 magrets or duck breasts (about 13 ounces/370 g each)

1 tablespoon edible lavender

2 teaspoons coriander seeds

2 teaspoons cumin seeds

1 teaspoon fine sea salt

1 teaspoon finely grated lemon zest

Fleur de sel and freshly ground black pepper

Begin at least 2½ hours before serving. Score the skin of the magrets, without going all the way to the flesh, in a crosshatch pattern.

In a spice grinder or with a mortar and pestle, finely grind the lavender, coriander, cumin, and fine sea salt. Stir in the lemon zest. Rub all over the magrets. Wrap and refrigerate for at least 2 hours or overnight. Remove from the fridge and unwrap 30 minutes before cooking.

Preheat the oven to 425°F (220°C).

Put a large ovenproof cast-iron pan over medium-high heat. Add the magrets skin side down and cook until the skin is browned and crisp, about 10 minutes. Flip the magrets and baste with the juices. Transfer the pan to the oven and roast for 15 minutes. A meat thermometer inserted into the thickest part should register 135°F (57°C) for medium-rare meat (pink in the center), which is my preference. The official food safety recommendation is 165°F (74°C), yielding well-done meat.

Transfer to a cutting board, preferably one with grooves around the edges to collect the juices. Cover with foil and let rest for 5 to 10 minutes.

Cut at a diagonal into slices ½ inch (1.25 cm) thick. Transfer to a warmed serving platter, keeping the breast shape intact, then fan the slices slightly to expose the meat. Drizzle with the juices, sprinkle with fleur de sel and black pepper, and serve.

ONE OF MY FAVORITE BUTCHERS IN PARIS IS AT THE ALL-ORGANIC BATIGNOLLES market, where growers and breeders drive in from nearby farms on Saturday mornings. A matronly woman comes with her teenaged daughter and a pimpled apprentice to sell meat she raises and butchers herself, and always has the right cut for my needs. If it's a roast I'm getting, her young employee will tie it up painstakingly as we discuss the details of the *bœuf en croûte* I plan to serve.

This French Beef Wellington will make you flush with pride, yet is not at all hard to pull off. Brown the roast, cook some mushrooms, wrap them up in puff pastry, put your handiwork in the oven . . . and out comes a gorgeously browned bœuf en croûte for you to slice at the table, basking in your friends' oohs and aahs. Or, if your friends are French, in their *ohlalas!* and *ouaaaahs!*

2 tablespoons olive oil

1¾ pounds (800 g) boneless beef roast, tied and patted dry

1 teaspoon fine sea salt

²/₃ pound (300 g) brown mushrooms, finely chopped

1 tablespoon freshly squeezed lemon juice

¼ cup (15 g) chopped fresh flat-leaf parsley

Easy Puff Pastry (page 105) or 12 ounces (340 g) store-bought all-butter puff pastry

Egg wash: 1 large egg lightly beaten with 1 teaspoon water

· VARIATION ·
To make individual bœufs en croûte, slice the seared roast into 6 thick steaks, divide the dough into 6 pieces, then assemble 6 bundles. Bake for 20 to 25 minutes.

Begin at least 3 hours (and up to 10 hours) before serving. In a heavy-bottomed skillet, heat 1 tablespoon of the olive oil over medium heat. Cook the roast to brown on all sides, about 15 minutes, turning every few minutes. Season with ½ teaspoon of the salt. Set aside on a rack to cool completely; discard the string.

Add the remaining 1 tablespoon olive oil to the skillet and set again over medium-high heat. Add the mushrooms, lemon juice, and remaining ½ teaspoon salt. Scrape the browned bits from the bottom and cook until the mushrooms are tender and the liquids are evaporated, about 10 minutes. Remove from the heat, stir in the parsley, taste, and adjust the seasoning. Let cool completely.

Line a baking sheet with parchment paper.

(recipe continues)

Set aside 1½ ounces (40 g) of the puff pastry in the refrigerator. On a lightly floured work surface, roll out the remaining puff pastry into an oval or rectangle 2 inches (5 cm) longer than your roast at each end and about 3½ times its width. Spread half the mushrooms in the center of the dough to mimic the shape of your roast and brush the rest of the surface with some of the egg wash.

Put the roast on top of the mushrooms, top with the remaining mushrooms, and wrap the pastry up and over the roast, pressing to seal. Place seam side down on the baking sheet. Brush with more of the egg wash.

Roll out the reserved puff pastry. Using a sharp knife or small cookie cutter, create decorative shapes and arrange them on the roast, covering tears as needed. I make pointy oval leaves and trace the veining with the dull side of my knife. Brush with the remaining egg wash. Refrigerate for at least 1 hour or up to 8.

Remove from the refrigerator while you preheat the oven to 475°F (250°C).

Bake until golden brown, 25 to 30 minutes. Transfer to a cutting board and let rest 10 minutes. Slice with a serrated knife and serve.

CHRISTOPHE BEAUFRONT, PART OF THE INITIAL WAVE OF *BISTRONOMIE* CHEFS (see page 13), opened his restaurant L'Avant-Goût ("foretaste") in the mid-nineties and soon made a name for himself with his pork pot-au-feu. The traditional pot-au-feu (literally, "pot over fire") is a stew of beef (the less noble cuts) and winter vegetables (potatoes, carrots, leeks, turnips, celeriac). His reimagined version features lots of warm spices and an unusual but winning combo of fennel and sweet potato. In the spirit of the original dish, he uses lesser cuts of the animal, including pigs' tails and pigs' ears, but the recipe can be made with more easily found cuts, preferably a mix.

This is a hearty dish for a tableful of hungry friends. It is best served in two installments, as is customary for pot-au-feu: First, offer bowls of the broth with crusty bread; next, the stew itself, with meat and vegetables, strong mustard, and pickles.

~POT-AU-FEU~
de cochon aux épices

PORK POT-AU-FEU WITH WARM SPICES

SERVES 6

1 tablespoon olive oil

3½ pounds (1.5 kg) pork (parts suitable for braising, preferably a mix: spare ribs, shoulder, shank, cheeks . . . bone-in where applicable)

2 medium carrots, peeled and cut into 1-inch (2.5 cm) lengths

2 leeks, split lengthwise, carefully rinsed for sand, and cut into 1-inch (2.5 cm) slices

1 medium yellow onion, peeled and cut into 8 wedges

4 garlic cloves, peeled

1½ teaspoons fine sea salt

¼ teaspoon coriander seeds

¼ teaspoon juniper berries

¼ teaspoon black peppercorns

¼ teaspoon ground ginger

2 whole cloves

1 whole star anise

2-inch (5 cm) cinnamon stick

3 cups (750 ml) dry white wine or vegetable stock

2 medium bulbs fennel (about 1¼ pounds/550 g), trimmed, cored, and cut into ¾-inch (2 cm) slices

1 large sweet potato, peeled and cut into ¾-inch (2 cm) cubes

Finely chopped fresh flat-leaf parsley leaves, for serving

Crusty bread, for serving

Strong Dijon mustard, for serving

Quick Red Onion Pickle (page 19) or cornichons, for serving

In a large heavy pot, heat the oil over medium-high heat. Working in batches if necessary, add the pork in a single layer and cook until browned all over, 3 to 5 minutes per side. When all the pork is browned, return all to the pot. Add the carrots, leeks, onion, garlic, 1 teaspoon of the salt, the coriander, juniper berries, peppercorns, ginger, cloves,

(recipe continues)

star anise, and cinnamon stick. Pour in the wine, scrape up any bits from the bottom of the pot, and top up with water as needed to barely cover. Cover, bring to a simmer over medium heat, and simmer until the meat is very tender, about 4 hours, stirring from time to time and adding more boiling water if the level gets too low.

About 30 minutes before the pork is done, in a medium saucepan, combine the fennel, sweet potato, and remaining ½ teaspoon salt. Add 2 cups (480 ml) of the cooking liquid from the pork (no need to replace it with water). Cover, bring to a simmer over medium heat, and cook until tender, about 20 minutes, stirring regularly.

When the pork is done, remove the meat from the pot and cut into 2-inch (5 cm) cubes. Strain the broth through a fine-mesh sieve. Discard the solids and return the broth to the pot.

To serve, ladle some of the broth into cups or bowls, sprinkle with parsley, and serve with crusty bread. (Return the meat and vegetables to the remaining broth and keep warm.) After everyone has had the broth, arrange the meat and vegetables in the center of a large serving platter and pour some of the remaining broth over the meat. Serve with mustard and onion pickle or cornichons.

OFFAL

LES ABATS IS AN UMBRELLA TERM FOR ANY EDIBLE PART OF AN ANIMAL
that is neither muscle nor bone: brain, liver, cheek, tongue, snout, ear,
foot, tail, sweetbread, kidney, heart (technically a muscle, but still considered an abat), testicles, head, tripe . . .

If you couldn't make it through the end of the list, you are not alone.
These foods are probably the most divisive of all; people either adore or
detest them. Yet they are an important part of the history of Parisian
cuisine: These lesser cuts were often the only ones the working class
could afford, and their richness in nutrients played a major role in public health. The dishes featuring them in restaurants were referred to as
plats canailles; the wealthy liked the thrill of *s'encanailler,* mingling
with the riffraff to eat them.

Organ meats went out of style in the later part of the twentieth century,
as industrialized farming practices made noble cuts more widely acces-
sible (for better or for worse) and mad cow disease scared off some eat-
ers. *Triperies*—butcher shops specializing in offal—all but disappeared.

But the gastro-bistro movement (see page 13) revived the passion, as
chefs welcomed the creative challenge of preparing these low-cost ingredients in delicious ways. Availability outside of France can be a challenge, so I haven't included offal recipes in this book; but when you make
it to Paris, I hope you give them a chance.

ONE OF THE MOST SIGNIFICANT DIFFERENCES BETWEEN RESTAURANT cooking and home-style cooking in France is the use of sauces. Chefs make them naturally—no bigger deal than breathing—while amateurs sometimes shy away from them, resisting the thought of one more thing to prepare. Yet if you become the sort of cook who can whip up a few simple sauces, you'll bring your cooking to a whole new level. This one is based on mirepoix—the holy trinity of onion, carrot, and celery—and hard apple cider. It cooks down to a richly aromatic sauce that works wonders on roasted pork. It is an easy dish to prepare for a dinner party.

~FILET MIGNON~
de porc rôti, sauce au cidre

ROASTED PORK
TENDERLOIN WITH APPLE CIDER SAUCE

SERVES 6

2 pounds (900 g) pork tenderloin, cut into 4 pieces

1 teaspoon fine sea salt

5 ounces (140 g) bacon, finely diced (see Note, page 61)

¼ medium yellow onion (60 g), finely diced

½ small carrot (30 g), peeled and finely diced

⅓ stalk celery (30 g), finely diced

1½ cups (360 ml) hard cider

1 bay leaf

¼ cup (60 ml) crème fraîche or full-fat sour cream

Freshly ground black pepper

Chopped fresh chervil or flat-leaf parsley, for serving

Steamed rice or potatoes, for serving

At least 2 hours or the day before serving, rub the pork with 1 teaspoon salt. Wrap tightly and refrigerate for 1½ hours or overnight. Remove from the refrigerator 30 minutes before cooking.

Preheat the oven to 400°F (200°C).

In a large saucepan, cook the bacon over medium heat until browned, about 5 minutes, stirring often. Remove the bacon. Pour the rendered fat into a bowl and set aside. Add the onion, carrot, and celery to the pan, cover, and cook until the vegetables soften, about 5 minutes. Add the cider and bay leaf and simmer, uncovered, until reduced by half, 20 to 25 minutes. Strain and return to the cleaned saucepan; discard the solids. Keep warm over low heat.

Meanwhile, in an ovenproof cast-iron skillet large enough to accommodate the meat, heat the reserved bacon fat over medium-high heat. Add the pork and brown on all sides, about 10 minutes. Transfer to the oven and roast until a meat thermometer inserted into the middle of a piece registers 145°F (63°C), 15 to 20 minutes. Transfer to a cutting board, cover with foil, and let rest for 10 minutes.

Just before serving, whisk the crème fraîche into the warm pan sauce. Slice the meat into 1½-inch (4 cm) slices. Arrange on a serving dish, spoon the sauce on top, and sprinkle with black pepper and chervil. Serve with rice or potatoes.

THERE ARE ALWAYS AT LEAST THREE BUTCHERS ON HAND WHEN YOU WALK into Jacky's *boucherie* on the cobblestoned rue des Abbesses, in Montmartre. Any one of them will prepare your meat with skill and care, but if it happens to be Jacky taking your order, you're in for a real treat.

Beaming from behind the counter, arms folded across his chest, Jacky first demands to know what you are planning to make with the meat. Once you tell him, he exclaims "*Impeccable!*" with a wink before getting to work. You *could* opt out of sharing that information, but it would be a subtle slight, a refusal to dance the dance that makes interactions with French food vendors so rewarding.

Jacky places the meat on the scale and looks up with a proud smile ("Ha!") when the weight reaches the exact amount you requested. He then slices, dices, rolls, butterflies, ties—anything you ask. Savvy French cooks know to take advantage of this to save time and effort at home.

This lamb recipe gives me the opportunity to participate in this entire exchange, as Jacky debones and trims the shoulder to order. A simple paste of mustard, honey, and thyme spread over the meat creates a wonderful caramelly finish. It is Jacky-approved. He would also join me, I am sure, in recommending a side of mashed potatoes and Brussels sprouts.

~ÉPAULE~
d'agneau roulée à la
moutarde et au miel

ROLLED
LAMB
SHOULDER
WITH MUSTARD
& HONEY

SERVES 4

· NOTES ·

This is a great Easter dish, best eaten the day it is made.

You can roast two lamb shoulders at a time to feed a larger group. Pick a baking dish roomy enough to accommodate them without crowding.

3 tablespoons strong Dijon mustard	1 teaspoon fine sea salt
2 tablespoons honey	3 pounds (1.3 kg) boneless lamb shoulder
2 teaspoons dried thyme	Fleur de sel and freshly ground black pepper

Begin the day before serving. In a small bowl, stir together the mustard, honey, thyme, and fine sea salt. Lay the lamb shoulder out on a large plate and coat both sides with the mustard mixture. You'll find that the lamb shoulder has a neat side and a messier side where it was deboned. Roll it up into a roast so the neat side faces out and secure with a few pieces of kitchen twine. Wrap up in the butcher's paper or plastic wrap and refrigerate overnight.

About 3½ hours before serving, preheat the oven to 300°F (150°C). Take the lamb shoulder out of the fridge, put it in a baking dish in which it fits just comfortably, and cover loosely with foil.

Transfer to the preheated oven and bake, basting with the juices every now and again, until the meat is well browned and the juices are dark and caramelized, about 3 hours.

Transfer to a cutting board, preferably one with grooves around the edges to collect the juices. Discard the twine. Cut the meat into ½-inch (1.25 cm) slices and transfer to a warmed serving platter. Drizzle with the cooking juices, sprinkle with fleur de sel and black pepper, and serve.

~HÜNKAR BEĞENDI~

TURKISH LAMB
WITH
EGGPLANT

SERVES 4

RUE DU FAUBOURG-SAINT-DENIS IS ONE OF PARIS'S MOST DIVERSE MARKET streets, and one of my favorites. Filled with shops, restaurants, and cafés, it is crowded at all hours of the day and night. Here, two worlds meet: communities of working-class immigrants, who come here to work, shop, and socialize, and a young urban artsy crowd that is driving the gentrification of the neighborhood.

Everywhere you look, there is a bistro, hole-in-the-wall, or take-out stand beckoning you to taste its offerings. The variety of street foods reflects the multinational mix of people who hang out here, and you can travel the world from Syria to India by way of Corsica in just a few steps.

At the top of the street, right by the monumental Porte Saint-Denis arch, is a handsome restaurant showcasing traditional Turkish cuisine. This is where I first tasted *hünkar beğendi*, a classic dish of slow-cooked lamb served over a roasted eggplant and cheese sauce. The name means "sultan's delight" and it is indeed a flavorful dish worthy of royalty that will be just as appreciated by your nonroyal friends.

---

3 medium eggplants
(about 3 pounds/1.4 kg total)

Olive oil

1½ pounds (650 g) boneless
lamb shoulder, cut into 1-inch
(2.5 cm) cubes

1 medium yellow onion,
finely diced

2 garlic cloves, minced

Fine sea salt

3 medium tomatoes
(about 1 pound/450 g total), diced

2 teaspoons fresh oregano leaves,
chopped, or ½ teaspoon dried

½ teaspoon ground cinnamon

¼ cup (35 g) all-purpose flour

1 cup (240 ml) milk (any kind)

3½ ounces (100 g) freshly
grated Turkish kasseri cheese
or provolone

A handful of fresh flat-leaf parsley,
chopped, for serving

1 lemon, cut into 4 wedges,
for serving

Cooked bulgur, for serving

Preheat the oven to 400°F (200°C).

Pierce the eggplants a few times with a knife and put on a rimmed baking sheet. Roast until dark and completely soft, about 1 hour, flipping halfway through. Let rest until cool enough to handle.

MEANWHILE, COOK THE LAMB: In a heavy-bottomed pot, heat 1 tablespoon olive oil. Add the lamb, onion, garlic, and 1 teaspoon salt. Cook, stirring frequently, until the onion is softened and the meat is browned on all sides, about 10 minutes. Stir in the tomatoes, oregano, and cinnamon. Cover and simmer until the sauce is silky and the meat is tender, about 50 minutes. Taste and adjust the seasoning. (The meat can be cooked a day ahead; the flavor will improve. Cover and refrigerate overnight. Reheat before proceeding.)

Scoop the eggplant flesh into a blender or food processor, discarding the skin. Process until finely puréed.

In a large skillet, heat 2 tablespoons olive oil over medium heat. Stir in the flour and cook 2 to 3 minutes, stirring with a spatula, until foamy. (This is a *roux blanc*.) Add the puréed eggplant, then stir the milk in slowly. Cook until thickened, a few more minutes. Remove from the heat and fold in the kasseri. Taste and adjust the seasoning. (You can prepare the eggplant sauce up to a day ahead. Cover and refrigerate, and reheat before proceeding.)

Scoop the sauce onto plates, top with meat, and sprinkle with parsley. Serve immediately, with lemon wedges to squeeze and bulgur on the side.

TROUT
WITH ZUCCHINI
&
ALMOND CREAM

SERVES 4

I REMEMBER THE FIRST TIME I HAD DINNER AT YARD, A POCKET-SIZE restaurant located in a then-unfamiliar area of the 11th arrondissement. I thrilled as we approached: cobblestoned alleys, artists' workshops, and everywhere a stylish crowd spilling out of bars and cafés, enjoying one another's company and the low evening sun. I looked at them and caught a whiff of an alternate life path, one in which I would live in this hidden gem of a neighborhood and meet with my friends here on the regular.

Yard would be a favorite, with its unpretentious atmosphere and tight seating that prompts intertable conversations, and its open kitchen, delivering the produce-driven cuisine I adore. One standout dish was trout with slim grilled zucchini and almond cream, a modern riff on trout amandine; I would have licked the plate clean, but the crusty bread volunteered to mop up the sauce. Serve as a first course or light main; add roasted fingerling potatoes to make it more filling.

¼ cup (60 ml) almond butter

1 garlic clove, finely chopped

1 tablespoon plus 1 teaspoon freshly squeezed lemon juice

Fine sea salt

2 cups (30 g) arugula

4 teaspoons olive oil

2 small zucchini

1 pound (450 g) skin-on trout fillets

¼ cup almonds (35 g), toasted and roughly chopped

In a small bowl, combine the almond butter, garlic, 1 tablespoon of the lemon juice, and ¼ teaspoon salt. Add cold water, 1 tablespoon at a time, until you get a creamy consistency, about 3 tablespoons total.

In a medium bowl, toss the arugula with 1 teaspoon of the olive oil, the remaining 1 teaspoon lemon juice, and a pinch of salt.

Halve the zucchini lengthwise, and then again, to get 4 long pieces of zucchini. Cut each at an angle into two shorter sections.

In a griddle or skillet, heat 2 teaspoons oil over medium-high heat. Add the zucchini, sprinkle with ¼ teaspoon salt, and cook for 2 minutes on one cut side, without moving, until golden. Flip to the other cut side and cook another 2 minutes without moving. The zucchini should be al dente. Transfer to a covered bowl to keep warm.

Wipe the griddle clean and heat the remaining 1 teaspoon oil over medium heat. Add the trout skin side down, sprinkle with ¼ teaspoon salt, and cook for 4 to 6 minutes to rare; adjust the cooking time to the thickness of your fillets. Cut the fillets into sections.

On each of 4 plates, spoon 2 tablespoons almond sauce to form a round, slightly off-center. Alternate stacks of zucchini, trout, and arugula in the center of the plate, as if building a campfire. Sprinkle with the almonds and serve.

MY APARTMENT IS CLOSE TO LA GOUTTE D'OR ("THE GOLDEN DROP") AND Château-Rouge ("red castle"), neighborhoods where large communities of African immigrants live, and where no-frills restaurants serve a simple, family-style cuisine. These are mostly frequented by locals so the food hasn't been dumbed down for Westerners, and short of traveling abroad in person, they're a fine opportunity to get a taste of Senegal, Togo, or Mali.

One of the dishes seen on most menus is *mafé*, a stew of meat or fish in peanut sauce that is popular across West Africa and also goes by the name of *azindéssi* or *tigua degué*. The sauce is simply made by thickening the stew with peanut butter. This version of mafé, with fish and spinach, is quick to prepare, and makes for an incredibly flavorful, satisfying dinner. I serve it over bowls of rice; traditional alternatives include *fonio* (a type of millet), couscous, *fufu* (a cassava mash), sweet potatoes, and plantains.

~MAFÉ~
de poisson aux épinards

PEANUT
FISH STEW
WITH SPINACH

SERVES 4

1 tablespoon neutral oil, such as sunflower seed, grapeseed, or canola

1 medium yellow onion, finely diced

2 garlic cloves, finely minced

Fine sea salt

¼ cup (60 ml) smooth peanut butter

1 small red chile pepper, finely diced (seeded to lessen the heat)

1 vegetable bouillon cube (see Notes)

1 bay leaf

3 cups (720 ml) simmering water

1 (14-ounce/400 g) jar or can of whole peeled tomatoes, drained

1 pound (450 g) fresh spinach, roughly chopped, or 10 ounces frozen spinach, thawed, squeezed, and roughly chopped

1½ pounds (700 g) sustainably sourced white fish of your choice, cut into 1-inch (2.5 cm) cubes

Freshly ground black pepper

Steamed white rice, for serving

· NOTES ·

African cooks make frequent use of bouillon cubes. If you prefer not to, use 3 cups vegetable stock instead; add it in place of the simmering water.

This works well as a soup instead of a stew; add a little more liquid to get the consistency you like and adjust the seasoning accordingly.

In a large, heavy-bottomed pot, heat the oil over medium heat. Add the onion, garlic, and ½ teaspoon salt and cook, stirring frequently, until softened, about 2 minutes. Add the peanut butter, chile pepper, bouillon cube, bay leaf, and ½ teaspoon salt. Stir in 1 cup (240 ml) of the simmering water. Add the tomatoes and crush roughly with a spatula. Add the remaining 2 cups (480 ml) simmering water, bring to a simmer, and cook 20 minutes. Add the spinach and fish and simmer until the spinach is wilted and the fish is just cooked through, about 5 minutes.

Sprinkle with black pepper, taste, and adjust the seasoning. Serve over steamed white rice.

~POISSON~
au beurre blanc

FISH
BEURRE BLANC

SERVES 4 TO 6

I WASN'T PARTICULARLY FOND OF FISH WHEN I WAS A CHILD, BUT MY mother had a magic trick to make me eat it: She whipped up a quick beurre blanc sauce, buttery and lemony, that elevated any fillet she had selected from the fish stall. I have a vivid memory of the white ceramic pan she used, tilting it for easier whisking, and the hollow scraping sound of the spoon as she scooped it onto each serving.

Beurre blanc fully deserves its place in the pantheon of classic French sauces. The method is fast and straightforward. I like to offer steamed potatoes or rice and a seasonal green vegetable on the side, as they benefit from a spoonful of the beurre blanc as well.

· **NOTE** ·

If you prefer a smooth sauce, strain it to remove the bits of shallots before adding the herbs.

6 ounces (170 g) shallots, finely chopped or grated

⅓ cup (80 ml) dry white wine

3 tablespoons freshly squeezed lemon juice

1 teaspoon fine sea salt

1 tablespoon olive oil

1½ pounds (700 g) fillets (½ to ¾ inch/1.25 to 2 cm thick) sustainably sourced fish of your choice

6 tablespoons (85 g) unsalted butter, diced

6 tablespoons (90 ml) heavy cream

⅓ cup (20 g) finely chopped fresh herbs, such as chives, flat-leaf parsley, cilantro, chervil, or sorrel

In a medium saucepan, combine the shallots, wine, lemon juice, salt, and ⅓ cup (80 ml) water. Bring to a simmer over medium heat and cook stirring every once in a while, until the shallots are soft and the liquid is reduced by about half, about 5 minutes.

Meanwhile, in a large skillet, heat the oil over medium heat. Add the fish and cook until just cooked through, 2 to 3 minutes on each side.

As soon as the shallot mixture is reduced, add the butter little by little, whisking constantly to emulsify. Whisk in the cream. Keep the sauce warm as the fish finishes cooking.

Stir the herbs into the sauce just before serving. Arrange the fish in a serving dish, or divide among plates, and spoon over the sauce. Serve immediately.

BURGUNDY, A SHORT EASTWARD TRAIN RIDE FROM PARIS, IS A REGION known for its wines, its colorful rooftop tiles, its strong, sneeze-inducing mustard from the city of Dijon, and, of course, *bœuf bourguignon*. This slow-simmered beef and wine dish is iconic French comfort food.

As Paris becomes more vegan- and vegetarian-friendly, plant-based versions of this classic pop up on restaurant menus around the city, often starring mushrooms in place of the beef. They turn this into a completely different dish, but their meatiness and my secret ingredient—a spoonful of miso paste—work to create the same kind of hearty, savory effect in what is, in short, a very good mushroom stew.

Bœuf bourguignon is often served with mashed or boiled potatoes, but since this dish already contains potatoes for body and substance, I serve it instead with cauliflower mash. Mushrooms don't require as much simmering as beef does, so this goes from chopping to serving in about an hour—just enough time to sample the rest of that bottle of Pinot Noir.

~CHAMPIGNONS~
façon bœuf bourguignon

MUSHROOM BOURGUIGNON

SERVES 6 AS A MAIN

1 tablespoon olive oil

1 medium yellow onion, minced

3 medium carrots, peeled and cut into ⅓-inch (1 cm) slices

2 garlic cloves, minced

2 teaspoons fresh thyme or 1 teaspoon dried

1½ teaspoons fine sea salt

4 medium potatoes (about 1½ pounds/600 g total), peeled and cut into ½-inch (1.25 cm) cubes

1 tablespoon miso

2 bay leaves

1½ cups (360 ml) medium-bodied dry red wine, such as a good Pinot Noir

2¼ pounds (1 kg) brown mushrooms, trimmed and cut into 1-inch (2.5 cm) pieces

Slurry: 1 tablespoon arrowroot or tapioca starch (see Note), combined with 1 tablespoon cold water

¼ cup (15 g) packed fresh flat-leaf parsley leaves, roughly chopped

Freshly ground black pepper

Cauliflower mash, for serving

· NOTE ·
You can use cornstarch for your slurry in a pinch. But for acidic sauces, wine-based in particular, arrowroot and tapioca starch are more effective.

In a large heavy-bottomed pot, heat the olive oil over medium heat. Add the onion, carrots, garlic, thyme, and salt and cook, stirring regularly, until softened, about 8 minutes. Add the potatoes, miso, and bay leaves. Pour in the wine, stir to combine, and cover. Bring to a simmer and cook for 15 minutes.

Stir in the mushrooms, return to a simmer, and cook uncovered, stirring regularly, until all the vegetables are cooked through, 15 to 20 minutes. Discard the bay leaves. Stir in the slurry and simmer until the sauce is slightly thickened, about 5 more minutes.

Taste and adjust the seasoning. Transfer to a serving dish, sprinkle with parsley and black pepper, and serve with mashed cauliflower.

~RATATOUILLE~
au four

OVEN-ROASTED
RATATOUILLE

SERVES 6 AS A SIDE DISH

I AM THE PROUD GRANDDAUGHTER OF A FABULOUS COOK WHO LIVED IN Provence for much of her adult life and spoke with exquisite fondness of the summer vegetables that she bought at her village market—how she cooked each separately and with loving care until they glistened with her good olive oil, and reunited in the pot like long-lost friends.

But my grandmother was not a snob, and she didn't think less of me when I laughed and confessed that I make "ratatouille" by arranging all the vegetables on a baking sheet and letting the oven do the work for me. While unconventional, this method yields stupendous results: almost sweet ratatouille, with a wonderful roasted flavor, the texture so rich and pleasing it feels like dessert.

I eat this with Steamed Hard-Boiled Eggs (page 62), their velvety yolks melding with the juicy vegetables. It is also an easygoing side that goes with everything, from grilled meats to steamed fish to pasta and brown rice.

· NOTES ·

As a further departure from the classic, I sometimes add a lemon (preferably organic), sliced into 8 wedges, to roast with the vegetables.

Ratatouille is even better the next day, and it freezes well, too.

2 medium eggplants, cut into ¾-inch (2 cm) cubes

2 medium zucchini, cut into ¾-inch (2 cm) cubes

4 tomatoes, cut into ¾-inch (2 cm) cubes

1 red bell pepper, sliced

1 medium yellow onion, finely diced

2 garlic cloves, smashed and peeled

2 sprigs fresh rosemary or ½ teaspoon dried

2 sprigs fresh thyme or ½ teaspoon dried

¼ cup (60 ml) olive oil

1½ teaspoons fine sea salt

Fresh basil, for serving (optional)

Preheat the oven to 350°F (175°C).

Put the eggplants, zucchini, tomatoes, bell pepper, onion, garlic, rosemary, and thyme on a large rimmed baking sheet. Drizzle with the olive oil, sprinkle with the salt, and toss well with your hands. Hide the garlic under the vegetables so it won't burn. Cover loosely with foil and bake for 45 minutes. At this point, the vegetables should be cooked through but not colored. Remove the foil and bake for another 30 minutes, keeping an eye on the progress, until the vegetables have browned to your liking.

Remove the herb sprigs and serve, warm or at room temperature, with fresh basil if desired.

FRENCH ENDIVE CASSEROLE

FRENCH ENDIVES ARE IN SEASON THROUGHOUT THE COLDER MONTHS, from November to March. If you're ever shopping for them at a Parisian greenmarket during that time, don't get discouraged if you don't spot the snug, mini torpedo shapes right away. Look instead for crates covered with dark blue paper: It's a trick to protect the endives from the light, preventing photosynthesis so they will remain their desirable shade of white.

I like a good shaved endive salad, especially with walnuts and orange segments, as featured in my *French Market Cookbook*. But for something warm and comforting, I go back to a childhood dish I did not, in fact, enjoy as a child, but developed an appreciation for as an adult: the *gratin d'endives*, in which steamed endives are put to bed in a baking dish under a cover of béchamel sauce, sprinkled with cheese, and baked until browned and bubbling. The cheese and béchamel counterbalance the slight bitterness of the endives quite gracefully. This is a classic French recipe that is a wonderful complement to chicken or fish, or can be served as a vegetarian main, with a green salad.

2¼ pounds (1 kg) French or Belgian endives

4 teaspoons (20 g) unsalted butter

2 tablespoons (15 g) all-purpose flour

1 cup (240 ml) whole milk

1 teaspoon fine sea salt

½ teaspoon freshly grated nutmeg

Freshly grated black pepper

⅔ cup (65 g) freshly grated cheese, such as Comté or Gruyère

· **NOTE** ·

The gratin can be assembled ahead; keep it in the fridge and slip into the oven 30 minutes before dinnertime.

· **VARIATIONS** ·

Endives au jambon is another classic: Wrap each steamed endive in a strip of cooked ham before you put it in the dish. You will need about 12 ounces (340 g) thinly sliced ham.

This method can be applied to other cooked vegetables, such as cauliflower or mushrooms.

Rinse the endives and remove the core (this is where the bitterness lies). In a steamer, cook until tender, 12 to 15 minutes. Arrange in a snug layer in a medium baking dish.

Preheat the oven to 400°F (200°C).

Meanwhile, in a small saucepan, melt the butter over medium heat. Add the flour, stir it in quickly with a wooden spoon, and cook 2 to 3 minutes, stirring constantly, without coloring (this is *roux blanc*). Remove the pan from the heat, add a splash of the milk, and whisk it in until the roux is smooth.

Whisk in the rest of the milk over medium heat, a little at a time. Bring to a gentle simmer and cook, whisking constantly, until the sauce is thickened and velvety, 5 to 7 minutes. Remove from the heat, season with salt, nutmeg, and pepper to taste. Taste and adjust the seasoning.

Pour evenly over the endives, spreading with a spatula as needed. Sprinkle with the cheese and bake until bubbling and golden brown, about 20 minutes. Let set for 10 minutes before serving.

~POMMES ANNA~
au beurre noisette

BROWN BUTTER
POMMES
ANNA

SERVES 4 TO 6 AS A SIDE

ONCE LOCATED ON BOULEVARD DES ITALIENS, LE CAFÉ ANGLAIS DOMINATED Paris's social and culinary scene in the nineteenth century, thanks to its rarefied atmosphere and visionary chef, Adolphe Dugléré, who had trained under Antonin Carême. The restaurant closed on the eve of World War I, but its legacy lives on in literature—in the work of Zola, Flaubert, Maupassant, and Proust—and through the chef's creations. The most famous is probably Pommes Anna, named in honor of a famous courtesan who frequented the restaurant, Anna Deslions.

It is rare to find this dish on the menu at Parisian restaurants nowadays, which is a shame. Pommes Anna is a study in simplicity and sophistication: Thin slices of potatoes are arranged in a spiral pattern, each layer brushed with melted butter and sprinkled with salt, then baked until golden. I gild the lily by using brown butter, which adds a nutty flavor.

2½ pounds (1.2 kg)
waxy potatoes, peeled

5 tablespoons (70 g) unsalted butter

1½ teaspoons fine sea salt

Preheat the oven to 425°F (220°C).

Using a sharp knife or mandoline, slice the potatoes ⅛ inch (4 mm) thick. (Do not rinse or soak the slices; the starch is what binds the layers.)

In a small saucepan, melt the butter over medium heat and cook, swirling the pan, to get it to the brown butter stage: First, the butter will boil in large bubbles. Soon, the bubbles will get smaller, the pitch of the boil will get higher, and the butter will turn light brown and smell nutty. At this point take off the heat immediately and pour into a bowl. (If you overcook the butter, the solids will burn and form black, acrid-tasting flakes. Throw it out and start again; it's happened to the best of us.)

Grease the bottom of a shallow 10-inch (25 cm) ovenproof cast-iron pan with some of the brown butter. Cover the bottom of the pan with one-third of the potato slices, arranging them in a slightly overlapping, circular pattern. Brush with one-third of the remaining butter and sprinkle with ½ teaspoon of the salt. Make two more layers using the remaining potatoes, butter, and salt. Set over medium heat and cook, without disturbing, to initiate browning on the bottom, 10 minutes. Cover loosely with foil, transfer to the oven, and bake for 30 minutes. Remove the foil and bake until the potatoes are cooked through (a knife should pierce through easily) and the top is browned and crusty, 20 to 30 minutes. Let rest for 10 minutes on the counter.

Run a spatula around the edges and underneath to loosen and flip carefully onto a serving plate so the golden bottom faces up. If any of the potatoes are stuck to the bottom of the pan, scrape them off and return them to where they belong. (If you don't feel up for the flipping, it is fine to serve the potatoes directly from the pan.) Slice into wedges and serve.

PARISIANS HAVE A PASSION FOR WHAT THEY CALL *BO BUN*, BUT IS REALLY *bún bò nam bộ*, a Vietnamese salad of rice vermicelli, crudités, and marinated beef. Finished with chopped peanuts, lots of sliced mint, and a sweet-and-sour dressing, it is an explosion of textures and flavors that are especially satisfying when you get home from work late and tired and ravenous, and the Vietnamese takeout around the corner is making eyes at you. When you have just a little more time, make it at home for a casual dinner. Most of the prep can be done ahead, so all that is left to do is sear the meat and assemble the bowls.

FOR THE MARINATED BEEF

1 pound (450 g) beef steak, such as flank or top round, sliced across the grain into very thin strips

2 stalks lemongrass

2 garlic cloves, finely chopped

1½ tablespoons fish sauce

1 tablespoon turbinado sugar

½ teaspoon fine sea salt

FOR THE SAUCE

¼ cup (50 g) turbinado sugar

¼ cup (60 ml) boiling water

¼ cup (60 ml) fish sauce

¼ cup (60 ml) rice vinegar

2 tablespoons freshly squeezed lime juice

½ teaspoon chili-garlic sauce, such as Sriracha

2 garlic cloves, finely chopped

FOR COOKING AND ASSEMBLING

8 ounces (225 g) rice vermicelli noodles

3½ ounces (100 g) lettuce, roughly chopped

1 medium carrot, peeled and grated or julienned

½ medium cucumber (unpeeled), cut into thin sticks

1½ cups (80 g) bean sprouts

1 tablespoon neutral oil, such as sunflower seed, grapeseed, or canola

½ medium yellow onion, thinly sliced

8 store-bought spring rolls (variety of your choice), reheated according to package directions (optional)

1 small red chile pepper (optional), thinly sliced (seeded for less heat)

⅓ cup (55 g) salted roasted peanuts, chopped

16 fresh mint leaves, thinly sliced

AT LEAST 2 HOURS AHEAD OR THE DAY BEFORE SERVING, MARINATE THE BEEF: Put the slices in a medium nonreactive bowl. Trim the root end of the lemongrass and remove the fibrous outer layers (save for

(recipe continues)

lemongrass tea or making stock) to expose the tender, waxy middle, like a thin pencil. Slice finely. Add the lemongrass, garlic, fish sauce, sugar, and salt to the beef. Stir to coat, cover, and refrigerate.

HOW TO PREPARE RICE VERMICELLI NOODLES

Soak the noodles in cold water for 20 minutes. Transfer to a large pan and add water to cover. Bring to a simmer and cook until tender, about 10 minutes. Drain, rinse with cold water, and drain again. The noodles can be prepared up to 1 hour in advance. When ready to use them, if they are sticking together, rinse again with cold water and drain well.

PREPARE THE SAUCE UP TO 1 DAY BEFORE SERVING: In a medium bowl, stir together the sugar and boiling water. Stir in the fish sauce, rice vinegar, lime juice, chili sauce, and garlic. Let stand at room temperature while you prepare the rest of the recipe. (If making more than 1 hour ahead, cover and refrigerate.)

Prepare the noodles according to the package directions (or see How to Prepare Rice Vermicelli Noodles, left).

Set out 4 large bowls. Put the chopped lettuce and noodles at the bottom, then the grated carrot, cucumber sticks, and bean sprouts in three piles. The bowls can be prepared up to 1 hour before serving; keep at cool room temperature.

JUST BEFORE SERVING: In a skillet, heat the neutral oil over medium-high heat. Add the onion and cook, stirring frequently, until softened and lightly golden, about 2 minutes. Add the beef and marinade and cook, stirring regularly, until the beef is just cooked through, about 3 minutes.

Divide the meat and juices among the bowls. If including spring rolls, cut each into three pieces using kitchen shears and distribute among the bowls. Sprinkle with the sliced chile (if using), peanuts, and mint. Drizzle each bowl with 3 tablespoons of the sauce and serve with chopsticks, instructing guests to combine all the ingredients.

LA MAISON VÉROT

⩴ Three Generations of Charcuterie Makers ⩴

GILLES VÉROT IS A PROUD THIRD-GENERATION *CHARCUTIER.* HIS grandparents started a thriving shop in the center of Saint-Étienne (a city near Lyon) in 1930, and his father and uncle took over in the sixties. The young Gilles grew up in the boutique, surrounded by terrines and sausages, and knew as early as age ten that he, too, would follow in the family business.

He had the opportunity to apprentice in Lyon and Paris, and fell for the excitement the capital city offered. He married the daughter of his mentor, and together they started their own shop on rue Notre-Dame-des-Champs in 1997, in the iconic Saint-Germain-des-Prés neighborhood.

He has been a leading figure of the charcuterie scene ever since, winning multiple awards—including the prestigious *Championnat du monde de pâté en croûte* (world championship of French meat pie) and the *Championnat de France du fromage de tête* (French championship of head cheese)—and generally advocating for quality and authenticity.

His display is enough to make your head spin, your eyes darting from dish to dish, each celebrating a different regional style (Parisian, Lyonnaise, Alsatian, Breton, and Norman) and together forming a mouthwatering Tour de France. Sausages galore, Parisian ham, *pâté lorrain,* duck galantine, rabbit terrine, pike quenelles, breaded pork feet . . . all of them made fresh and in-house.

For Gilles Vérot, the future of charcuterie lies in being transparent about the ingredients and sourcing; in refining beloved classics to keep up with modern tastes and generating excitement with new creations and limited editions; and in breaking free from the limitations of a boutique to present his products in other contexts—in wine bars (see page 166), in prestigious hotels, at brunches around the city.

In fact, Vérot's know-how has traveled across the ocean: He formed a partnership with Daniel Boulud in New York City, and for a decade they have been producing French charcuterie locally (using small-farm, U.S.-bred pork) and serving them at the chef's establishments.

PEARS
POACHED
IN SPICED
RED WINE

SERVES 6

THIS GORGEOUS DESSERT SHOWS UP LIKE CLOCKWORK ON BISTRO menus in Paris every fall, and remains popular through the end of winter, showcasing different varieties and shapes of pear, as the months go by: Guyot, Comice, Passe-Crassane, Conférence . . .

It's an easy make-ahead treat when friends are coming over to dinner, and the spiced wine makes my apartment smell like a Christmas market. I serve the poached pears with a little crème fraîche, soon stained purple from the wine sauce, and a bowl of butter cookies, such as Caramelized Arlette Cookies (page 239), for crunch.

Mixed with dry white wine and a dash of dark rum, the strained poaching wine can be turned into a delicious cocktail to greet guests and make them forget the grim weather outside.

· NOTES ·

Use an entry-level red; your best bottle would not shine here.

Good kinds of pears to use here include Bosc, Bartlett, or Anjou, but I also encourage you to seek out lesser known, locally grown varieties.

The pears can be served as an accompaniment to a cheese platter.

· VARIATION ·

You can make this recipe in the summer with peaches or nectarines.

6 medium pears (see Notes), ripe but still firm

3 cups (750 ml) red wine (see Notes)

¾ cup (150 g) sugar

Zest of 1 lemon, in strips

Zest of 1 orange, in strips

1 cinnamon stick

1 whole star anise

Seeds from 2 green cardamom pods

3 whole cloves

½ cup (120 g) crème fraîche, for serving

Caramelized Arlette Cookies (page 239) or store-bought butter cookies, for serving

Cook the pears the day before serving. Peel them, carve out the core with a melon baller, and slice the base horizontally so they'll stand upright when served.

In a large saucepan, combine the wine, 1 cup (240 ml) water, the sugar, lemon zest, orange zest, cinnamon, star anise, cardamom, and cloves. Bring to a simmer over medium heat. Lower the pears in, laying them on their sides, and cook at a low simmer for 20 minutes, turning the pears regularly. Let cool to room temperature in the poaching liquid. Cover and refrigerate until the next day. Remove from the refrigerator 1 hour before serving.

Stand the pears upright in a wide serving bowl and pour in a shallow pool of the spiced wine. (Reserve the rest of the wine to make a cocktail.) Serve with a dollop of crème fraîche per guest, and Caramelized Arlettes.

ON THE BUSY CENTRAL SIDEWALK OF BOULEVARD DE CLICHY, THERE IS a little snack stand that sells various kinds of candy and churns fresh pralines all day long. The smell of these peanuts slowly roasting in caramelizing sugar is so strong and so pervasive it slips right through the air vents of the metro underneath. Unsuspecting travelers exchange childlike smiles when the automatic doors open at the Blanche metro station and a waft of caramel comes rushing in.

These *chouchous* are a traditional treat found at any fun fair or Christmas market in France and are as unintimidating as candy-making will ever get. I make mine with mixed nuts and find it has many uses besides topping Creamy Rice Pudding (page 240): I snack on it with squares of very dark chocolate, sprinkle it on Vanilla Ice Cream (page 246), and package it up as pretty holiday gifts for my sons' teachers.

~NOUGATINE~
aux fruits secs mélangés

MIXED NUT
BRITTLE

MAKES 4 CUPS (480 G)

1⅓ cups (100 g) sliced almonds

¾ cup (100 g) raw pistachios

¾ cup (100 g) raw peanuts

¼ teaspoon fine sea salt

4 tablespoons (55 g) unsalted butter

¾ cup (150 g) sugar

· NOTES ·

If you can only find salted and roasted pistachios and/or peanuts, you can use them, but skip the salt.

Mix and match with whatever nuts you have available. Make sure to chop any bigger nuts to (roughly) peanut size.

Line a baking sheet with parchment paper or a silicone baking mat.

In a bowl, combine the almonds, pistachios, peanuts, and salt.

In a medium saucepan, melt the butter over medium heat. Add the sugar, stir, and cook, stirring constantly, until you get a creamy, light brown caramel, 3 to 5 minutes. Stir the nuts into the caramel and cook, stirring constantly, until the mixture comes together and forms a mass, 2 to 3 minutes. Pour onto the prepared baking sheet, spread with a spatula, and let harden completely at room temperature.

Break into pieces, large or small; use your fingers or chop roughly with a knife. Store in an airtight container at cool room temperature for up to 1 month.

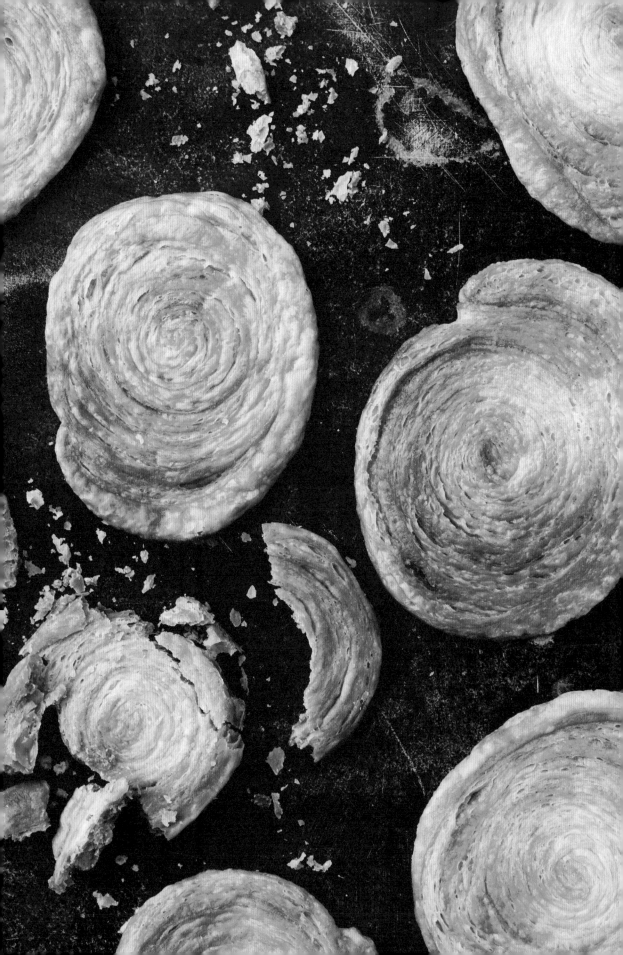

I FIRST DISCOVERED *ARLETTES*—A FRENCH GIRL'S NAME WHOSE POPULARITY peaked around World War II—at a now-defunct pastry shop in the Batignolles neighborhood. I fell in love with the spiral puff pastry confections, distant cousins of the elephant's ear cookie, and soon learned to make them at home.

Arlettes are a quick win of a cookie: Roll up some puff pastry into a tight log, cut into thickish slices, dust liberally with powdered sugar, and flatten out into slender oval shapes with a rolling pin. These bake into buttery and impossibly crisp cookies, shiny with a caramelized glaze. Serve them with tea or coffee in the afternoon, and use them to adorn fruit desserts or a simple cup of Vanilla Ice Cream (page 246).

Powdered sugar

Easy Puff Pastry (page 105),
or 12 ounces (340 g)
store-bought puff pastry

Dust your counter and rolling pin with powdered sugar and roll out the puff pastry to form a rectangle about ¼ inch (6 mm) thick. Starting at a short side, roll the dough tightly on itself to form a log. Wrap in parchment paper and put in the freezer for 20 to 30 minutes to firm it up enough to slice neatly with a knife.

Preheat the oven to 350°F (175°C) and line a baking sheet with parchment paper. Have ready a second sheet of parchment paper and a second baking sheet that nests into the first.

Using a sharp knife, cut the dough log crosswise into ½-inch (1.25 cm) slices. Dust the counter and rolling pin again with powdered sugar and roll each slice out with a back-and-forth motion (not side to side) to form an elongated oval about ¼ inch (6 mm) thick. Arrange on the prepared baking sheet. Top with parchment paper and the second baking sheet (this is to prevent puffing up). Bake until golden brown, 15 to 18 minutes. Transfer to a rack to cool completely.

~ARLETTES~
caramélisées

CARAMELIZED ARLETTE COOKIES

MAKES 20

· NOTE ·
It is easier to handle the puff pastry in a cool kitchen.

~RIZ~
au lait crémeux

CREAMY
RICE
PUDDING

SERVES 6 TO 8

L'AMI JEAN IS A RESTAURANT IN THE 7TH ARRONDISSEMENT RUN BY Stéphane Jégo, a tattooed and bearded chef in his mid-forties. Jégo came to Paris from Brittany, got his culinary mind blown working for a decade with Yves Camdeborde, the founding father of *bistronomie* (see page 13), and then fifteen years ago struck out on his own.

Dinner at L'Ami Jean means a boisterous evening in tightly packed quarters, eating bold dishes that leave you with a silly grin on your face. Just when you think you can't possibly eat another bite, in comes Jégo's signature dessert, an old-fashioned rice pudding inspired by his mother Philomène's. It is served family-style, a big bowl of creamy *riz au lait*, with a cup of salted caramel mousse to spoon on top and a cup of pecan *nougatine*—caramelized brittle—for sprinkling.

Rice pudding is a good make-ahead dessert, easy and comforting. I don't make it quite so over-the-top but have taken a few pages from L'Ami Jean's book: I fold a bit of whipped cream into the cooked rice for a lighter, smoother texture and offer it with nougatine, a crunchy note that jazzes up the dish.

· NOTES ·

It is essential to use short-grain white rice here, not parboiled or precooked. That is the only kind that will split and release its starch to create a creamy texture.

I can see your mind racing with the different spices and flavorings you could spike this with. I won't stop you, but remember, this is a rice pudding meant to evoke the simple flavors of childhood.

4 cups (960 ml) milk (any kind)

2/3 cup (135 g) short-grain white rice (no substitutions! See Notes)

1 vanilla bean, split lengthwise

½ cup (100 g) sugar

½ cup (120 ml) heavy cream, chilled

Mixed Nut Brittle (page 237), roughly chopped, for serving

Make the rice pudding 4 hours in advance, or the day before serving.

In a medium saucepan, combine the milk and rice. Scrape the vanilla seeds out of the vanilla bean and add them and the pod to the pan. Simmer, stirring occasionally, until the grains of rice have swollen and split, releasing their starch and creating a creamy texture, about 20 minutes. Taste to make sure the grains are soft; if not, cook a little longer. Stir in the sugar and cook until very creamy, 10 minutes longer. Transfer to a bowl and cover. Let cool completely and refrigerate until chilled. A skin will form as it cools; stir it back in.

In a bowl, with an electric mixer, whip the cream to form firm peaks. Fish the vanilla bean out of the pudding and discard. Using a spatula, stir in one-quarter of the whipped cream to loosen the texture. Fold in the remaining whipped cream in 3 additions, working the spatula in a circular vertical motion to keep as much volume as possible. (This can be prepared 4 hours ahead; cover and refrigerate.)

Spoon into serving bowls and serve with the brittle alongside.

Some restaurants in Paris just sweep you off your feet with the historic splendor of their décor. Brasserie Julien, just a few steps from the bustling Grands Boulevards, is one of them. Established in 1903, it has been attracting clients ever since, including Édith Piaf, one of their famous regulars. With its ornate art nouveau façade, *pâte de verre* painted ladies on the walls, gorgeous tiled floor depicting wildflowers, and stunning glass ceilings, it feels like a luxurious time machine, transporting you straight to turn-of-the-century Paris.

Suitably, the brasserie serves classic French dishes, and the profiteroles are a signature dessert. Order them and you'll get a bowl of three big puffs, filled with vanilla ice cream, over which your server will pour chocolate sauce from a metal spouted pot, in a mouthwatering spectacle.

It's a much easier dish to re-create than you would think, and so much wow for your efforts! Here, I'm providing recipes to make it completely from scratch, but you could certainly opt to make the puffs only, and use store-bought vanilla ice cream and chocolate sauce.

~PROFITEROLES~

VANILLA ICE CREAM PUFFS

WITH CHOCOLATE SAUCE

SERVES 6

Choux Pastry (recipe follows)

3 cups (720 ml) Vanilla Ice Cream (page 246), or store-bought

Simple Chocolate Sauce (page 247), or store-bought, warm

½ cup (35 g) sliced almonds, toasted

Make the choux pastry, transfer it to a piping bag fitted with a plain ½-inch (1.25 cm) tip, and refrigerate as directed. (This can be prepared up to 1 day before serving.)

Preheat the oven to 400°F (200°C) and line a baking sheet with parchment paper or a silicone baking mat.

Pipe the choux pastry into 18 mounds about 1½ inches (4 cm) in diameter, leaving about 1 inch (2.5 cm) of space in between. Smooth out the tops with the tines of a fork lightly dipped in water.

Bake until the puffs are browned all over (check the lower sides around the base especially), 25 to 30 minutes, rotating the baking sheet front to back after 10 minutes. Transfer to a rack to cool completely.

To assemble, use a serrated knife to slice the puffs horizontally in half, like a bun. Fill each with a scoop of vanilla ice cream and arrange in dessert bowls, 3 puffs per person. Bring to the table to finish in front of your guests: Drizzle with the warm chocolate sauce, sprinkle with sliced almonds, and serve.

· NOTES ·

If you pipe smaller puffs, about 1¼ inches (3 cm) in diameter, and sprinkle them with pearl sugar before baking, you'll have made *chouquettes* (sugar puffs), an afternoon treat popular with Parisian children. Pearl sugar is available from specialty baking stores and can be ordered online.

Uncooked puffs may be frozen. Put the baking sheet in the freezer for 2 hours, then transfer the puffs to a freezer bag. No thawing necessary; just bake for 30 to 35 minutes.

CHOUX PASTRY

Pâte à choux

**MAKES ABOUT
10½ OUNCES
(300 G), TO
MAKE ABOUT
20 MEDIUM
PUFFS**

IF YOU'RE AT ALL INTERESTED IN FRENCH CUISINE—a safe assumption if you're holding this book—you will not regret learning how to make choux pastry. This magical dough unlocks a world filled with *choux à la crème* (cream puffs), *chouquettes* (sugar puffs), éclairs, *religieuses*, profiteroles, and gougères (cheese puffs) of all stripes.

The key to choux pastry success is threefold. First, you'll have to cook the panade properly—full instructions below—to rid the pastry of excess moisture and ensure it rises properly in the oven. Second, the oven door must remain closed for the first half of the baking, to avoid deflating the puffs (sad face). Third and most important, you must have the courage to bake your choux pastry creations long enough for them to dry out so they won't soften and sag once cooled. This requires a little faith: When the puffs become brown, you will be tempted to remove them from the oven. But it will be too soon, and you will need to sit on your hands for a few more minutes. Only then will your puffs display the properly contrasted texture, crisp on the outside and impossibly moist inside.

2½ tablespoons (35 g) unsalted butter, diced

¼ teaspoon fine sea salt

½ cup (120 ml) milk, dairy (not skim) or nondairy (unflavored and unsweetened)

½ cup (65 g) all-purpose flour, sifted

2 large eggs

In a medium saucepan (not nonstick), combine the butter, salt, and milk and bring to a simmer over medium-low heat. Remove from the heat, add the flour all at once, and stir quickly with a wooden spoon until well blended and smooth. (This is your panade.)

Return the pan to medium-low heat and keep stirring until the dough is satiny and leaves a slight film at the bottom of the pan, about 5 minutes. Remove from the heat and let cool for 3 minutes. Add the eggs, one at a time, stirring well after each addition. Transfer to a piping bag or sturdy freezer bag and refrigerate for at least 1 hour or up to 1 day before piping and baking.

~CRÈME GLACÉE~
à la vanille

VANILLA
ICE CREAM

**MAKES ABOUT 3 CUPS
(720 ML)**

THE CLASSIC METHOD FOR MAKING FRENCH VANILLA ICE CREAM IS BASED on a simple crème anglaise, or vanilla custard. I happen to have a good family recipe for fail-safe crème anglaise, so naturally it is the process I use to make vanilla ice cream, too.

If you are a detail-oriented cook, you will notice two differences between my custard base here and the recipe I offer for crème anglaise on page 109. First, ice cream benefits from added fat to make the mouthfeel smoother, so I use a little cream in addition to the milk. And second, we perceive the sweetness of foods less when they are very cold, so I increase the amount of sugar slightly to get the level just right.

2 cups (480 ml) milk (not skim)	1 large egg
½ cup (120 ml) heavy cream	½ cup (100 g) sugar
1 vanilla bean, split lengthwise, or 2 teaspoons pure vanilla extract	3 tablespoons cornstarch

In a medium saucepan, combine the milk and cream. Scrape the vanilla seeds out of the vanilla bean and add them and the pod to the pan (or if using extract, add it now). Bring to a simmer over medium heat.

In a medium bowl, whisk together the egg and sugar. Whisk in the cornstarch until blended.

When the milk mixture simmers, remove the pan from the heat and whisk about ½ cup (120 ml) of the heated milk mixture into the egg mixture. Pour the combination back into the saucepan and return to medium-low heat. Cook, stirring constantly with a wooden spoon in a figure-eight motion. Scrape the bottom and sides of the pan well, and keep the heat low enough to prevent the milk from boiling. The custard is ready when it is thick enough to coat the spoon and your finger leaves a neat trace on the back of the spoon. It should take about 4 minutes.

Put a fine-mesh sieve over a clean medium bowl and pour the custard through it. Cover and let cool to room temperature for 2 hours on the counter, then refrigerate overnight. A skin will form; you can just whisk it back in.

Churn in an ice-cream maker according to the manufacturer's instructions.

PARISIAN SHOPKEEPERS TYPICALLY HAVE A STRONG SENSE OF PRIDE, but G. Detou tops them all with the bold pronouncement that they have everything (*"J'ai de tout"*). A few steps from rue Montorgueil, in the old neighborhood of Les Halles, it is a small shop for professional bakers and dedicated home cooks like my grandmother, a regular in her day.

One entire wall is dedicated to baking and couverture chocolate, displaying different cacao contents, origins, and manufacturers. I like to buy a large bag for the best rate, share it with a friend or neighbor, and keep a comfortable stash on hand for all my chocolate needs, including this simple chocolate sauce.

This is an easy basic to have in your repertoire, essential for making Profiteroles (page 243), but also for pouring over Buckwheat Crêpes (page 81) and Carousel Waffles (page 131), or drizzling over any cake that needs enhancing. As a bonus, it cools to a lovely ganache-like texture you can scoop into a quenelle shape (that's a pointy oval) and serve alongside a scoop of vanilla ice cream with a sprinkle of sliced almonds.

~SAUCE~
au chocolat toute simple

SIMPLE CHOCOLATE SAUCE

MAKES ABOUT 1½ CUPS (360 ML)

6 ounces (170 g) high-quality bittersweet chocolate (60 to 70% cacao), finely chopped

¾ cup (180 ml) milk (any kind)

⅓ cup (80 ml) heavy cream

In a medium saucepan, combine the chocolate, milk, and heavy cream. Set over low heat and cook, stirring gently but constantly with a spatula, until the chocolate is melted and the sauce smooth, not allowing the mixture to simmer, 4 to 5 minutes.

Use immediately or let cool and reheat gently just before serving.

LATE NIGHT

TARD DANS LA NUIT

Paris by night
au hasard de la nuit
qui nous prend par la main
—BÉNABAR

THERE IS A UNIQUE QUALITY TO PARIS IN THE WEE HOURS
of the morning, when partygoers spill out of bars and night-
clubs, chat and laugh with complete strangers, despair that
they've missed the last metro home, sit on curbs to gather
their thoughts, and decide they might as well get something
to eat.

Late-night options are limited in Paris. It's mostly greasy
kebab joints, popular with a not-too-discerning crowd. Those
with a sense of their city's history much prefer a good Parisian
Onion Soup.

PARISIAN ONION SOUP

SERVES 4

THE ONION SOUP HAS LONG BEEN A STAPLE OF FRENCH CUISINE: ONIONS are easy to grow, they keep well throughout the cold months, and cooking them low and slow in stock creates a restorative dish.

Alexandre Dumas offers seven versions in his *Grand Dictionnaire de Cuisine*, published posthumously in 1873. The one missing, inexplicably, is the *soupe à l'oignon gratinée,* an invention of Parisian cooks: In it the soup is topped with a slice of stale bread and cheese, and broiled until the cheese melts, creating divinely messy strands when the spoon digs out a bite.

In the second half of the nineteenth century, it was served at every brasserie in Les Halles throughout the night, when theater goers and party people crossed paths with the *forts des Halles,* the early-rising workmen charged with carrying heavy loads of merchandise to the food market. The former wanted to steady their stomach after all the drinking—the soup was therefore nicknamed *soupe à l'ivrogne,* drunkard soup—while the latter needed nourishment before a day of backbreaking labor.

A few establishments have kept Parisian onion soup on their menu to this day. Au Pied de Cochon is one of the rare restaurants in the city that remains open all night, serving their famous pork foot and their glorious onion soup to hungry souls, sober and not so much.

· NOTE ·

An (extra-fresh) raw egg yolk is sometimes added in the final moments of cooking for binding. This should not be served to children, pregnant women, or anyone with a compromised immune system.

1 tablespoon (15 g) unsalted butter

1 tablespoon olive oil

1¼ pounds (560 g) yellow onions, thinly sliced

1 teaspoon fine sea salt

2 tablespoons all-purpose flour

½ cup (120 ml) dry white wine (substitute beer, or half port wine, half water)

4 cups (960 ml) beef stock, preferably homemade

1 tablespoon red wine vinegar

4 slices crusty artisanal bread (about ½ inch/1.25 cm thick), trimmed as needed to fit in your soup bowls

1½ cups (150 g) freshly grated cheese, such as Comté or Gruyère

Freshly ground black pepper

Freshly grated nutmeg

In a heavy-bottomed pot, heat the butter and oil over medium-low heat. Add the onions and salt, stir to combine, and cook, stirring, until the onions are deeply caramelized, 30 to 35 minutes. If you find they are sticking to the bottom of the pot, add 1 tablespoon water and scrape off any stuck bits. Stir in the flour. Add the wine and stock, scrape the bottom of the pot, and bring to a simmer. Cover and cook 15 minutes. Stir in the vinegar, then taste and adjust the seasoning. (The soup base can be prepared up to 1 day ahead. Let cool, cover, and refrigerate. Reheat before continuing.)

Preheat the broiler.

Divide the soup among 4 heatproof bowls and put them on a rimmed baking sheet. Top each bowl with a slice of bread and sprinkle each with 6 tablespoons cheese. Put under the broiler, watching closely, until the cheese is golden and bubbling, 4 to 5 minutes. Sprinkle with black pepper and nutmeg.

Set the bowls on heatproof plates and bring to the table, warning your guests the bowls themselves will be piping hot.

ACKNOWLEDGMENTS

THIS BOOK HAS BEEN AN ABSOLUTE JOY to write, thanks in large part to my assistant and dear friend, Anne Elder. She was by my side every step of the way, in the kitchen and in the office, and brightened our every workday with her ideas, skills, and humor. If you hold the book close to your ear, I'm sure you can hear our laughter echoing through the pages.

Anne coordinated our amazing team of recipe testers, whom I owe a lifetime of gratitude. For their enthusiasm and commitment, and the invaluable feedback they shared, my thanks to Maura Atwater, Jordan Bacon, Judi Brown, Mary Sue Hayward, Jaclyn Kubik, Marci McCarthy, Valerie Michaleski, Judy Miller, Leigh Monichon, Sheri Nugent, Jenny Pearson-Millar, Anne Ritchings, Noel Roberts, Alison Rutherford, Sara Silm, Heather Stein Roberts, and Nathalie Wittemans.

I also want to thank the group of Chocolate & Zucchini superfans, who served as my board of advisers through the process, and all the readers of *Chocolate & Zucchini* who expressed excitement for this book along the way, giving me wings to make it the best book I could.

I had the good fortune of receiving insights and recipes from Bruno Brangea and Manon Fays (Champeaux), Gontran Cherrier and Benjamine Thomas, Catherine Cluizel, Forest Collins (52 Martinis), Corine and Gabrielle Di Ciaccio, Eric Frechon and Clarisse Ferreres-Frechon (Lazare), Romain Meder and Caroline Lefevre (Hotel Plaza Athénée), Adrian Moore (Hotel George V), Eric Ngo (La Cuisine Paris), Nicolas Pando (Comptoir Canailles), Apollonia Poilâne and Geneviève Brière, Nathalie Quatrehomme, Orr Shtuhl, Gilles Vérot, and David Valentin (Le Potager de Charlotte). I am immensely grateful for their time and generosity.

Mille mercis to Nicole Franzen for working her magic, shooting gorgeous pictures of my dishes and capturing the soul of my Paris with her camera. Much appreciation to Suzanne Lenzer and Andie McMahon for cooking and styling the food with such talent.

My thanks to Claudia Cross, my dream agent of fourteen years, and to the team at Clarkson Potter who made this book happen so smoothly and so beautifully: Amanda Englander, Andrea Portanova, Stephanie Huntwork, Aaron Wehner, Doris Cooper, Heather Williamson, Christine Tanigawa, Jen Wang, Jana Branson, Erica Gelbard, and Kevin Sweeting. Special thanks to my publishing heroine Rica Allannic.

Thank you to my mastermind partners Jane Bertch, Jules Clancy, Rachel Cunliffe, Anne Ditmayer, Judith de Graaff, Cécile Poignant, Darya Rose, and Catherine Taret, for cheering me on through the struggles and the wins, and making my life so much richer.

Caffeinated thanks to the lovely staff at Cuillier Abbesses, especially Andy, David, Mahela, and Yoann, for keeping my mug full as I typed away.

Thank you to my parents, Patrick and Sylvie, for making Paris my beloved birthplace and raising me on such good food.

Finally, all my love to Maxence, whom I married halfway through writing this book; and to Milan and Mika, *mes petits choux*.

INDEX

Fabien Courmont

CLOTILDE DUSOULIER is the creator of the award-winning food blog chocolateandzucchini.com, where she shares fresh, simple, and colorful recipes from her Parisian kitchen. She is the author of the cookbooks *Chocolate & Zucchini* and *The French Market Cookbook*, as well as the guide and reference books *Clotilde's Edible Adventures in Paris* and *Edible French*. She lives in Montmartre, in Paris, with her husband and two young sons.